LAND TENURE IN AN IBO VILLAGE IN SOUTH-EASTERN NIGERIA

LONDON SCHOOL OF ECONOMICS MONOGRAPHS ON SOCIAL ANTHROPOLOGY

The Monographs on Social Anthropology were established in 1940 and aim to publish results of modern anthropological research of primary interest to specialists.

The continuation of the series was made possible by a grant in aid from the Wenner-Gren Foundation for Anthropological Research, and more recently by a further grant from the Governors of the London School of Economics and Political Science. Income from sales is returned to a revolving fund to assist further publications.

The Monographs are under the direction of an Editorial Board associated with the Department of Anthropology of the London School of Economics and Political Science.

LAND TENURE IN AN IBO VILLAGE IN SOUTH-EASTERN NIGERIA

M. M. GREEN

LONDON SCHOOL OF ECONOMICS MONOGRAPHS ON SOCIAL ANTHROPOLOGY

Volume 6

Routledge
Taylor & Francis Group
LONDON AND NEW YORK

First published 1941 by Berg Publishers

Published 2020 by Routledge
2 Park Square, Milton Park, Abingdon, Oxon OX14 4RN
605 Third Avenue, New York, NY 10017

First issued in hardback 2021

Routledge is an imprint of the Taylor & Francis Group, an informa business

ISBN 13: 978-0-367-71696-7 (pbk)
ISBN 13: 978-1-84520-016-9 (hbk)

To
S.R.E.

This material on land tenure forms part of the data collected during two tours in Nigeria, between 1934 and 1937, while I was the holder of a Leverhulme Research Fellowship for anthropological work among the Ibo people. I should like to take this opportunity of thanking the Leverhulme Trustees for the opportunity they gave me of learning something about this African people.

I should like also to thank Dr. C.K.Meek for explaining to me, in a short talk before I started, the main lines of Ibo kinship and local grouping. His book was not then published but I found his information and his Intelligence Reports of great value.His generous interest has always given me much encouragement.

I had not seen his work on Ibo land tenure before collecting my own evidence, but was confirmed in my findings by meeting his before writing up my material.

FOREWORD.

NAMES AND ORTHOGRAPHY.

For the spelling of Ibo words other than place names I have followed the orthography adopted by the Government Translation Bureau. For place names I have tried to follow the most common usage found in maps, in order to avoid confusion.

The word Ibo has established itself so widely in this form that I have used it rather than the more phonetically correct form, Igbo.

For tone markings I have used the system of Dr.I.C.Ward's "Introduction to the Ibo Language".

As the information in this paper was given me on the understanding that I was a private individual and not a government official I have omitted the real names of land owners and used symbols - A^1 C^1 etc. - instead. The genealogical tables at the end[1] show the extended families and land owning groups to which the individuals belong. They also show their relationship within the extended families though I would not in all cases vouch for their accuracy.

1. See p.60-63.

LAND TENURE IN AN IBO VILLAGE

CONTENTS

I INTRODUCTION.

A description of land tenure and of the ownership of the produce of land is apt to read as a tedious catalogue of facts. There was however nothing of indifference or boredom in the atmosphere in which the facts were collected. Land is, to the Ibo, a sensitive point which the enquirer has only to touch to get a reaction of suspicion and alarm. And palm trees are included with the land as subjects for anxiety. Moreover in Agbaja the pressure of population on land was considerable.

During the first six months that I spent in the village of Umueke Agbaja, in 1935, I hardly touched openly on the question of land tenure but observed and learned what I could incidentally. When I returned in 1937 for a further six months and determined to try a more systematic study I had to proceed with care. Remembering the experience of surveyors in other areas I never openly measured land. Pacing it unobserved and trying to count the paces, with passers-by saying "good morning" every few yards, is a less simple matter than it might appear. But it is better than nothing. Discretion was needed also about asking many direct questions unless one was sure of one's audience. My experience, in fact, confirmed what I have heard of that of forestry officers and surveyors as to the care needing in handling the question of land in the eastern provinces of Southern Nigeria.

This paper concerns the village of Umueke Agbaja. I have sometimes added points, and have specified that I was doing so, from other areas of Ibo country. And even a limited knowledge of such areas enables one to see that many of the features of land tenure in Umueke are found elsewhere. But no claim is made to deal with more than this village and that not exhaustively. Moreover, since it was in a rural area, the complicated problems that arise in townships like Onitsha are left aside. My reason for collecting together my notes on such a small area is that generalisation about things Ibo is impossible until facts have been collected from a sufficient number of separate localities. One also hopes that any set of local facts will form some sort of a basis of comparison for other areas and make their study simpler. I also found among government officials a feeling that no information about land, however small, was to be despised and that details were worth recording.

I therefore set down such information as I have got for what it is worth. To give substance to the description of how land is held it has been necessary to give some account of how it is used. Particularly in the case of woman, to omit any picture of their relationship to the land just because they do not own it would have been to present Hamlet without the Prince of Denmark. And this involved some reference to the relative positions of men and women as owners of the produce of the land. But no attempt is made to give any account of agriculture, whether of its technical methods or of its magico - religious ritual. That would be a separate undertaking.

The information here has been collected in a variety of ways. Some is based on observation, some on the day to day comments of people using the land, some on conversations with a number of informants. Some, as will appear in the text, on the statement of a single informant or on the contradictory accounts of two or more people. That the information is always accurate I cannot hope, particularly when only one person is the source. Informants vary in reliability and no one who has dealt with them will consider even the best, nor their interlocutor, infallible. Among those I have quoted in the text, C[1], whom I used a good deal because he was accessible, was of moderate accuracy and intelligence only. D[4] on the other hand was intelligent, objective and free from fear. Both were young men though C[1] was the senior member of his land owning group. As the subject of land was a jumpy one I tended to talk to the younger men rather than the elders about it. I talked to women of all ages about their connection with the matter. I put forward the picture as it painted itself. I hope that it does not in essentials deviate from the situation it depicts.

II THE VILLAGE OF UMUEKE AGBAJA

Before going on to land tenure itself it is necessary to describe shortly the main features of the community within which it was studied and to give a rough definition of terms. European words for Ibo local and kinship groups have been used in so many different senses by different writers that one can only choose the terms that seem most suitable and try to make clear what is meant by them. It will perhaps be suggested that a better plan would be to use the Ibo terms with full explanations of their meaning. But the Ibo use many of their words just as loosely as we do in English when we speak of place, family, home. Each may have half a dozen meanings and only the context can tell which is indicated in any particular place. Also Ibo words for social groupings are apt to be very local in range and therefore confusing for general purposes.

The locality described in this paper is what I have called the village of Umueke Agbaja[1]. It is one of eleven villages which together make up the village group of Agbaja which lies in the forest just to the south east of Umuduru in the south of Okigwi division. I use the word village group for Agbaja in the same sense that Dr. Meek uses it for Owerri though the less satisfactory word town has often been used for both. And just as Owerri is made up of five villages so Agbaja contains eleven, though of a much more rural character.

In Agbaja each village is a scatter of house groups and not a compact, walled circle of houses as is the case in and near Owerri. And the villages forming the village group are themselves scattered over a considerable area with tracts of bush in between them though two villages may sometimes be contiguous. Each village has a path, ceremonially cleared once a year, leading to the central market place of Agbaja.

By a house group is meant a collection of separate mud houses belonging to the individuals of an extended family. Sometimes two or more house groups are close together though not necessarily closely related; others are more widely separated. Some are compact; some have outlying houses several hundred yards away from the main settlement. As in many things Ibo there is no strict conformity to pattern.

---

1 It might, I believe, sometimes be called a compound in official reports.

By an extended family is meant a group of closely related people known by a common name and consisting usually of a man and his wives and children, his sons' wives and children, his brothers and half-brothers and their wives and children and possibly other near relatives. There is considerable variety of size.

All the people born in the village believe themselves to be descended ultimately from a common ancestor. In the same way, all the eleven villages of Agbaja claim a common mythical ancestor and both village and village group are thus kinship as well as local units. The villages also, besides having their own subordinate deities, acknowledge the central Agbaja deity. But in everyday affairs each village is largely an independent unit managing its own affairs, and within the village the various extended families tend to the characteristic Ibo awareness of difference rather than identity.

The village of Umueke Agbaja is an exogamous unit as the villages almost always are. In addition it does not intermarry with the next door Agbaja village of Umuecele which is considered nearly related. But it can marry anywhere else inside or outside Agbaja.

The form of dual division so often found in Ibo social grouping occurs in Agbaja which is divided into Agbaja-ama containing seven villages and Agbaja-owɛrɛ containing four. The villages also have this feature and Umueke consists of Umueke-ama and Umueke-owɛrɛ, each half claiming to be descended from a different wife of the same father. The origins of this system have been much discussed. Whatever they may be, its present form plays an interesting part in social organisation to-day. As however this has no direct bearing on land tenure it cannot be discussed here. But to avoid confusion it must be explained that the original division of Umueke was at some former time modified because the people of Umueke-owɛrɛ had become much more numerous than those of Umueke-ama. Since one of the uses of the dual division is the equal sharing of communal work it is important that the two groups should be as nearly numerically equal as possible. One of the extended families of Umueke-owɛrɛ, known as Umunwaebodim - a very large extended family at the present day - was therefore given to Umueke-ama for all such purposes of organisation. This has resulted in a confusion of terminology. When people now speak of Umueke-ama one always has to make sure whether they mean the original group, which feels itself to be one since it is descended from one mother, or this group plus Umunwaebodim. The latter equally feels itself in sympathy with Umueke-owɛrɛ. In this paper and in the maps the word Umueke-ama refers to the smaller, original group.[1]

At a rough estimate I should say that Umueke had about 300 to 400 inhabitants. In this village group of Agbaja, though the population is

---

See large separate map of Umueke-ama at end for different forms of house groups C and D.

The word 'brother' is used of those having the same father and mother 'Half brother' is used of those having the same father but different mothers.

1. See Map. p.42.

not as dense as in some parts of Ibo country, it is none the less reckoned at about 450 to the square mile.[1] This means a considerable pressure of people on the land. And from this pressure have developed the various means, discussed later, by which certain rights over land can be temporarily transferred from one person to another whether by pledging or by different forms of what, for want of a better word, one must call leasing.

The villages of Agbaja vary considerably in the amount of land they possess and there is thus a good deal of this temporary transference of rights between the denser and less dense patches of population. Even within one village there are variations. In Umueke, for instance, the people of Umueke-ama had a good deal of relatively fertile land and used to pledge it or, alternatively, let it for a farming season, to the people of Umunwaebodim, who were short of land, or to a neighbouring village or even to the next door village group of Umunumu. On the other hand the people of Umueke-owerε had land which produced very poorly. They, and also the people of Umunwaebodim, used to go to the neighbouring village group of Nzerem, several miles away, and get land on pledge or on seasonal lease. It was fortunate for Agbaja that Nzerem to the east, towards the Imo River, had surplus land. There was a steady tendency for Agbaja to flow over and farm on Nzerem land, in spite of the distance.

It is not easy to say with accuracy even for the village of Umueke Agbaja what is the normal cycle of cultivation and fallow as it varied according to the quality of the land, the number of people in a particular land owning group and so on. I have heard A^3 say that he was just going to clear a piece of bush that had not been farmed for ten years. He had I think left it because he had a good deal of land in relation to to his requirements. He was young and unmarried. I have also seen land being farmed for the first time for seventeen years, according to the owner, B^4, because its productive powers were so small.[2] But such figures need taking with a grain of salt. In Umueke the formal farming cycle seemed to be three years - that is to say one year of cultivation followed by two years of fallow. The cultivation would often be a mixed crop of yam, coco yam, corn, vegetable and perhaps later cassava. The cassava crop was sometimes carried through both nominally fallow years, the bush being allowed, after the first, to come up with it.[3]

1, I quote from memory from an Intelligence Report, not having it by me. I am told that this official figure is an underestimate.

2. See genealogical tables pp, 38-41 for connotation of these symbols, A^3, B4 etc.

3. One awaits with interest the results of the experiments of the Agricultural Department at Umuahia as to the extent to which cassava exhausts the soil. If it is an exhausting crop it seems unfortunate that land carrying it should be reckoned as fallow. Cassava is a relatively new crop in this district and is being increasingly grown. Not only is its food value poor but it has certain toxic effects, It is however cheap and easy to grow and is thus unfortunately, popular.

I was told that in some parts of Agbaja other than Umueke land was farmed every other year, but I do not know how true this is.

As to the quality of the land in Umueke, my Owerri and Mbieri staff were openly scornful of the small yams produced. Their size may of course have been partly due to the species of yam planted. But if my own efforts at gardening are any criterion I should say that some of the soil, at any rate, was remarkably poor.

III MYTHICAL BASIS OF RIGHTS OVER LAND

In considering the fundamental facts of land tenure one has to ask what are the grounds, such for instance as conquest or original ownership, on which tradition bases the right of a group to its land. For herein is the ultimate basis of the present legal situation. A people will often possess what has been called a mythical charter of land ownership in which past history is so presented by tradition as to justify the claim of the group members to own the land. I never heard an Agbaja man explicitly volunteer any such justification. My impression was that he simply assumed that Agbaja land belonged to Agbaja people. But the right to the land is, I think, implicit in the myth which one meets repeatedly, that all Agbaja people are descended from one father, Ngalaba[1], and one mother, ɔkpe Itɛ[2]. In trying to discover whether they were held to be the first people who had ever occupied Agbaja and whether they were autocthonous or had come from elsewhere I got a variety of replies. The subject is a delicate one. A British political officer apparently once asked to see the bush dedicated to the ancestors and the people seem to have feared some sinister motive, and since then Agbaja people have been nervous as to the upshot of such enquiries. Either for this reason or because there is no very elaborately formulated myth it is not easy to get a coherent version of these ancestral figures. But the main features relevant to the land can be indicated. I never heard anything to suggest, as in so many myths, that the ancestors had migrated from elsewhere and had then settled in Agbaja. It was just said that having been created by Ci (˙) and Ɛkɛ (˙.) they had first lived at Orie Ekpa, the middle of Agbaja, and now the site of its central market and of the shrine of one of its principal deities. One informant said that the ancestors "came out" - that is to say originated - there. Another informant said that they were the first people to come to Agbaja. When I asked if they found any one else living there when they came he said no - tradition said that they were the first inhabitants. I then asked whether this meant that they owned the land and whether present day Agbaja people own it by right of inheritance from these, their

---

1 Ngalaba means "branched" or "forked" and is sometimes used to mean a human being because he has two legs.

2 ɔkpe ITƐ means "a potter". Agbaja possesses clay suitable for potting and a certain number of pots are made there by the women.

original, ancestors. He at once said that this is so - a prudent answer but I believe a true one. And he went on to explain how information about titles to land is passed on from father to son so that each generation knows its own rights.

It is thus, I think, correct to say that the traditional right of the people of Agbaja to their land is implicitly backed by the myth of the original ancestors, from whose eleven sons the eleven villages of Agbaja are held to be descended.

IV OWNERSHIP TENURE IN UMUEKE AGBAJA

i) The landowning groups.

There are, as we have said, various tenures on which land can be held. But, with one exception, it can only be owned by the right of inheritance. The exception is that land held on pledge from one generation to another and unclaimed till all evidence of its original provenance is lost, comes to be looked on as the property of the heir or heirs of the man who originally obtained it on pledge. Apart from this the ownership of land is based on ancestral right.

A study of this ownership shows that the communal system which popular imagination associates with primitive societies, whereby a large number of people hold their land in common, is practically non-existent in Umueke Agbaja. There are, it is true, one or two small pieces of bush sacred to the chief village deities on which no one would ever farm. Thus, though I found no very definite theory of their ownership, they were, in practice, reserved for the community. And the same might be said of the small bit of bush in the centre of Agbaja, sacred to the original ancestors. I was also told that the ground where Agbaja used to expose its corpses before the Europeans introduced burial belonged to all Agbaja. Formerly no one would farm on it. Now however it is farmed by the villages near.

But generally speaking land is not communally owned by any large unit such as a village or village group. Nor does any of it lie about not belonging to anyone. It is divided up among small numbers of kinsmen, members of an extended family. The extended family of a house group is normally broken up into a number of smaller landowning groups each consisting of anything from one to half a dozen or more close male relatives some of whom may be children. The lines of division of the landowning groups follow those of kinship, the members of a group being more closely related to each other than to those of another group. This will be seen by reference to the genealogical tables of extended families A.B.C. and D at the end[1].

The whole of the extended family may often still own a tract of land in common known as their ALA OZUZU OHA (.'..'..)but except for this the landowning groups own their land independently.

---

[1] See infra pp.38-41.

Women do not own land. The village is an exogamous unit and a woman after marriage lives in her husband's village.

I never saw or heard anything to suggest that any right of ownership over the land was vested in any one who might be compared to a chief in other African societies, nor even in the council of elders of the village. When one reflects how control over the land, for instance in such matters as eviction, is one of the attributes and bases of chiefly power in some parts of Africa[1], one realises how the absence of any such centralised control of the land accords with, and reacts on, the democratic, pluralistic nature of Ibo social organisation. Ownership and control of the land are dispersed rather than concentrated, just as is authority in general social affairs.

It is, however, of the utmost importance to realise that though there is no large scale communal ownership of land there are none the less certain fundamental customary restrictions with regard to land. Europeans who have been used to thinking that African land tenure is communal are apt, when they find that this is only the case in a modified sense, to go to the other extreme and think that a state of complete individual ownership with the right of sale has practically been reached. This is, however, far from the facts. In the first place, though an individual may have considerable freedom of action with regard to the land - how much will emerge in the later discussion of various types of tenure - he nevertheless has co-owners whose rights cannot be ignored. In the second place, the sale of land, as distinct from pledging and leasing, is unequivocally forbidden by native law and custom. This was stoutly asserted not only for Umueke Agbaja but by my Mbieri interpreter about his own large village group, and he insisted that the law was universal among Ibo people. "Land cannot be lost" he said. Any assumption therefore by Europeans that land can be sold would cut right across one of the most fundamental bases of native society. The only title to permanent ownership of land is inheritance and even that title does not give the right to alienate the land irrevocably.

ii) Use of the Land. Apportionment for farming.

Speaking very roughly one can say that the land owned by the land-owning groups of an extended family tends to lie to some extent near the dwellings of the extended family. But it is not one compact area. If the house group has been moved, as is often the case, much of its land may be some distance away. It will also have many scattered plots some of which may, at some former time, have been acquired on pledge and have lapsed by default into its possession. The accompanying map of the land of the Umueke-ama division of Umueke, incomplete though it is, gives some idea of the way in which the land of even a small area is cut up and scattered about between different owners.

I See L.P.Mair. 'Chieftainship in Modern Africa, Vol.IX.No.3,p.308.

The chief boundary marks between the land of different owners are isolated trees. I have never in Umueke seen the low, earthed up ridges that sometimes in Owerri are used to delimit land.

Land is owned, as we have seen by small groups of kinsmen. But though the members of a group have certain communal rights over their land they do not form a common economic unit for the farming or the working of it. This is not the place to enter upon a description of farming nor of the reciprocal rights and duties of kinsfolk, but land tenure remains an empty concept without some brief description of how the land is used.

It would roughly be true to say that each man farms his share of the land himself and owns the produce himself. He may, and often does, call in a party of relatives or friends to help with the heavy work of bush clearing or hoeing and in return helps them another day. But this is merely a voluntary party and may or may not consist of other members of the land owning group. There is co-operative work between children and parents and between husbands and wives. But even so a husband and a wife will each own their crops individually and a man's son, as soon as he begins to grow up, will be given yams by his father and own his small crop though he will still help his father in farm work and give him palm wine on regular days. He will also until he marries be to a considerable extent fed by his mother.

So individual is the ownership of crops that members of the same land owning group will not only, as is customary, store their yams in separate divisions of the same ƆBA (˙·) - yam barn - but will sometimes have separate yam barns. These may even be away from their own house group and in some one else's. I knew one man of Umunwaebodim who owned land in common with two brothers of the same mother. But he stored his yams right away from theirs in the yam barn of a friend in Umueke-ama. And D^8 stored his yams away from his own land owning group and together with those of A^4. If therefore the land owning unit is small the unit which farms the land and owns the crops is smaller still, being really no more in the latter case than the individual. One should however add the qualification that the individual has certain customary obligations, such for instance as that of a woman to use her crops for feeding her husband and children and the husband to use his in helping to entertain guests.

Except for the garden outside the house, which the householder and his wife cultivate year after year, land is, in accordance with general Ibo custom, farmed for one season only and then allowed to go back to bush for a time, different land being cleared and farmed the following season.

One noticed in Umueke that when bush was cleared at the beginning of the farming season, though several people might clear adjacent plots, the tendency on the whole was for the new farms to be scattered about and not collected together in large areas as, for instance, in Owerri village group. I do not know how much consultation there was between the different land owning groups or even between all the members of one group as to where farming should be carried out in any one year. Such accounts as I got of farming arrangements did not mention any conferring except between father and sons or between full brothers in a group and I did not press the matter further. I quote some accounts that I was given, of concrete situations. One cannot of course generalise from any particular case and in things Ibo there is usually a considerable margin of variation. But one will gain an idea of the lines along which custom runs.

One sees for instance from the first two examples that custom regulates to some extent the areas within which the various members of a land owning group will farm at any time. There will not be a haphazard choice at the beginning of every season. The other examples show degrees of consultation between certain members of the landowning group at the beginning of each season. In the landowning group C^1 - C^4 of extended family C, C^1 told me that as he and his brothers C^2 and C^3 had a different father from C^4, their fathers being dead, they would continue to farm where their own father used to cultivate and C^4 would do likewise.[1] Thus although they all held their land in undivided ownership their use of it was restricted by following the use of their respective fathers.

If two or more men of the group are sons of the same father, the father being dead, they will, generally speaking, farm the land on which their respective mothers used, in the father's lifetime, to plant their crops, though they may sometimes agree to alter this plan. The arrangement is one of custom - OMƐNALA - (.'..) not of law - IWU (.'), said my informant, distinguishing clearly between the two, as people so often did.

Reference is made later to the way in which wives plant certain of their crops among their husband's yams. It is in places farmed thus that their sons will afterwards plant. It is because of this custom of farming on land where his dead mother used to plant crops that a man will sometimes say that he is planting on his mother's land. Until one grasps the custom one wonders what he means, since women do not own land. Here, as often with reference to land, it is easy to be misled by taking words at their literal face value.

In the case of the land owning group D^5 - D^{10} the group contained a father, D^5, with three sons, D^8, D^9 and D^{10}, old enough to farm for themselves. D^8, who was the only married son, told me that each year he and his brothers ask their father where they may farm and he tells them, except in the case of the bit of land immediately outside his own house which is his garden and which he knows he can plant each year. It is customary that sons who have a father alive should have their land for farming allotted to them thus by him.

As between sons of the same mother, she and the father being dead, there seemed to me to be no rigid rule. In the landowning group D^5 - D^{10} of extended family D, the wife of D^7, whom I met farming with her husband one day, told me that all the members of

---

1 See table p. 40.

the group just farm where they like each season without asking anyone i.e. without consulting the eldest member or each other. She then added that the piece of land I saw them hoeing then was regularly farmed by her husband every few years and none of the others would challenge his use of it. In other words her first remark evidently had to be understood in the light of her second - that customary use would temper the freedom of each to go where he liked. Later I asked D^8, the son of D^7's elder brother D^5, whether D^7 could clear land anywhere he liked at the beginning of each farming season without consulting his elder brother D^5. He said that he would consult D^5. The discrepancy between the view of D^8 and that of the wife of D^7 is obviously due to their different points of view. D^8 would tend to stress the rights of his father D^5 and the wife of D^7 would equally be concerned with those of D^7 and a difference of emphasis would result in a case where no rigid customary ruling seemed to stand.

In the other land owning group of this extended family, D^4 told me that if his elder brother D^3 were at home - he was usually away working - he would, at the beginning of the farming season, take palm wine for him and go to see him one evening, The elder brother would cook food for him and afterwards he would ask him what land he was to farm on that year. He added that he would first help his elder brother to cut bush and that two days later the elder would help him.

On the other hand, in the land owning group A^1 - A^4 of extended family A, A^3 told me that any of the four brothers - all of the same mother - could select the bit of bush he liked for clearing at the beginning of the farming season. He would talk to the eldest brother A^1 about it, but would not take him palm wine unless the land in question were a specially good bit - ISHI ALA ('`..) - head of the land -such as their father used to farm.

Evidently then with the usual Ibo lack of rigidity the procedure varies as between full brothers. The degree to which the elder will be consulted or all will go where they like or customary claims will be recognised will probably depend on the nature of the relations between the various people and on the amount and quality of land available. Friction unquestionably arises at times. I saw it repeatedly in the land owning group D^5 - D^{10} of extended family D. D^6 had died leaving no grown up son. He had been a policeman, which was a rare thing in Umueke since the older generation had had little to do with white men. But having been sold as a child he had been carried off into more sophisticated parts where he had got a job and where he married several Aro Cuku women. He eventually returned to his native village and died, leaving only young sons who were not old enough to stand up for their rights. But the widows, being Aro and strong minded, waged perpetual guerilla strife against what they comsidered the attempts of other members of the land owning group to encroach on their husband's land and to plant crops where they themselves thought they had a right to plant them.

But in the extended families of A and C which I knew fairly well, things apparently ran pretty smoothly so far as farming was concerned. And elsewhere in the village things seemed to be regulated with moderation and good sense within the various landowning groups. Disputes between groups as to boundaries are of course another matter. But I only remember one even of those in Umueke. Probably the land was densely enough populated to be divided up with the minimum of ambiguity as to boundaries.

Once when two members of a land owning group, a boy D^9 and his father's younger brother D^7, were disputing as to who should farm a particular plot, I heard the senior member of the group, D^5, admonishing D^7 and saying that he should not thwart D^9, since the boy was the reincarnation of their father's father. D^5 said afterwards to me that he himself would not try to seize and farm land where D^7 wished to farm since his own father had reincarnated in D^7. But though reincarnation is a recurrent theme in all Ibo life and though it does, as we note later, confer certain rights in the inheritance of property, it does not, I think, seriously enter into the farming arrangements of land. It is, rather, a sentimental consideration which would not weigh very heavily against more practical motives.

As we have said earlier an extended family is usually broken up into a number of land owning groups but it may still possess a tract of undivided land belonging in common to all the groups and known as ALA OZUZU ƆHA. But though owned in common it is not communally used any more than is the land of the land owning groups. Any individual of the extended family who likes can go and clear a bit of this ALA OZUZU ƆHA and plant his own crop. There is no gathering of the extended family at the beginning of the farming season to clear or share out the land.[1] All the extended families of Umueke have this reserve of undivided land with the exception of one, Umunwaebodim, which is a large "family" without very much land and all they have has been divided up.

iii) Inheritance and division of land.

Inheritance of a man's property, including land, is, in general principle, by his sons along the following lines.

---

1 In some other parts of Ibo country the practice is more communal. I was told, for instance, by an Mbieri man that in Mbieri some extended families, if they have a good deal of land, will have an undivided reserve like the ALA OZUZU ƆHA of Umueke. But at the beginning of the farming season the whole extended family will go and clear bush on this land and decide where each member shall plant on it. I asked if all would farm on it. He said not necessarily. But a 'wicked man' might get his share for the year and then lease it to someone else for the season and get rent which would be for himself alone. But at the end of the season the land he had leased would relapse again into the common reserve.

I have the impression too that in some other village groups there are, in certain cases, larger groups of people involved in the ownership and use of land than there are in Umueke Agbaya. But this needs confirmation.

If a man X has several wives, x^1, x^2, and x^3, the chief share of his land and other possessions will be inherited by his eldest son by whichever wife. This son is known as the DI OPARA(....)or, in Agbaja, the Di Okwara (....). If he should die his place as chief heir will be taken by his next brother of the same mother. Thus in Fig.I the chief heir will be the eldest son of x^1, the wife first married, But in Fig.II he will be the eldest son of x^2, the wife married second, since she was the first to produce a son. The next biggest share of the dead man's land or other property will go by custom to which ever son, by a different wife, is next in age. In Fig.I this will be the eldest son of x^3 and in Fig.II the eldest son of x^1. The third biggest share will go to which ever son, by a yet different wife, is next in age - in Fig.I this will be the eldest son of x^2 and in Fig.II the eldest son of x^3 - and so on, if there are more wives, until the eldest son of each wife, in descending order of age, has received his share. A smaller share still will then be given to the younger brother, same mother, of the eldest son of all. In Fig.I this will be the second son of x^1 and in Fig II the second son of x^2. Next, with a still smaller share, will come the younger brother, by the same mother, of the son who had second share. In Fig.I this will be the second son of x^3 and in Fig.II the second son of x^1. And so on till all the sons have had a share.

If it should happen that, for instance, the second son of the wife of the chief heir is younger than the second son of the wife of the second heir he will still take precedence of the latter.

FIG.I.

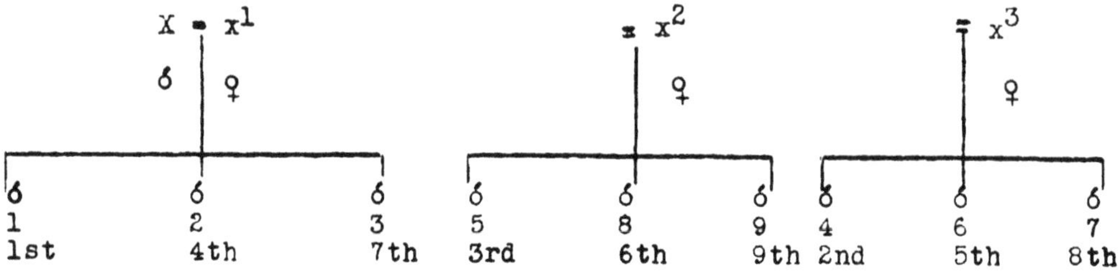

FIG.II

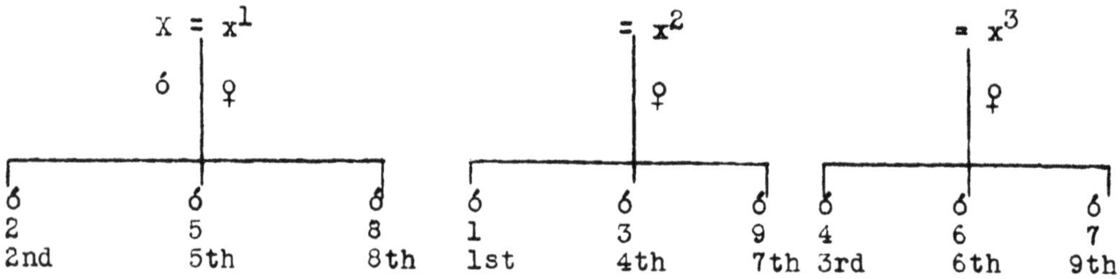

x^1, x^2, x^3 shows order in which wives married.
1st,2nd,3rd etc. shows order in which sons inherit.
1, 2, 3, etc. shows order of age of sons.
♂ denotes male.
♀ denotes female.

I was told by C^1 that if a man has no sons his younger brother of the same mother will inherit him, if he has one. A half brother by the same father will only inherit if he has no brother by the same mother. If he has neither full nor half brothers inheritance will be by a member of his ONAMA (˙˙.). The ONAMA was said to be a group of kinsfolk who could trace descent from one mother - that is to say from the wife of the same father. No question of matrilineal descent is involved. What it seems to mean is that a man who leaves neither sons nor brothers nor half brothers will normally be inherited by his nearest male kinsman, just as the husband of C^1 was inherited by C^5.

There arises of course the question of how far the wishes of the individual owner of property can modify customary rules of inheritance. One would not be surprised, among the Ibo, to find considerable evidence of individual variation and in fact there is I think, no doubt that it exists so far as personal property is concerned. We shall see this in connection with the inheritance of land held on pledge. But so far as ancestral land is concerned it is not easy to see how individual inclination can have much play. In the first place a man holds his land in common with the other members of his land owning group. At the time of his death it will not pass definitively to his sons or other heirs but will continue as the common property of the group, of which they form a part. It is only when the children of the group increase and grow up and marry that the need of dividing up the land will make itself felt. In the second place when the division is agreed upon it will be done publicly and ceremonially by the elders of the village according to the rules of inheritance. Individual wishes therefore seem to be largely ruled out.

It is interesting to notice that though the village does not, as we have seen, hold its land in common it none the less shows, in this question of dividing up the land of a group between its constituent members, that the question of land is one of general concern. C^1 gave me an account of the procedure. He said that if he and C^4 decided to divide up their land so that C^4 should own his separately from C^1 and his full brothers C^2 and C^3 they would have to summon four elders - NDI ƆHA (˙˙..) - from each division of Umueke, that is to say from Umueke-ama, Umunwaebodim and Umueke-owɛrɛ. They would bring food and palm wine for these elders, C^1 bringing more than C^4 since his father was older, and the elders would divide up the land among them according to custom.

Since the father of C^1 was older than that of C^4 the elders will tell C^1 to choose a piece of good land, ISHI ALA, that he would like for himself. What remains will be shared equally among them. C^1 will get no extra by reason of the fact that he has two brothers who will participate in his share. The respective ages of C^1 and C^4 will make no difference. If C^1 were younger than C^4 he would still get a larger share than C^4 since his father was older.

The whole occasion would be one of feasting and rejoicing since it is the entering into possession of one's own land. It is what the Ibo call IHƐ ƆGAƆGA (˙˙....) - a thing of pride - and would he ended with the customary shouts of TI HO! (˙.) which mark any such festivity.

The matter is clearly one of public importance since the land is the life blood of the community and its recognised delimitation essential. The summoning of the elders ensures, or should ensure, that all is done in accordance with right custom and that the whole affair is witnessed beyond any reasonable possibility of doubt.

In some cases land may be owned by several sons of one mother. C^1 told me that if, after getting his land divided from that of C^4, he and his brothers wanted at any future time to divide up their land they would only need to call the elders of Umueke-ama and not of all Umueke since they are all of the same mother. The customary method of division would be as follows.

In the first place the eldest son, in this case C^1, would get an eighth part of the whole land. As he put it, if his father's lands were eight he would get one. The remaining seven eighths would then be divided between the three sons. The land would of course be in scattered plots and each plot would be divided into three unequal shares, the eldest son C^1 getting the biggest, the next son C^2 the second biggest and the youngest son C^3 the smallest share. However small a plot of land might be - so it was affirmed - it would still be divided into three. This is to some extent borne out by the very small plots of land one sees being farmed often in this area. I did not ascertain whether this system of dividing each piece of land was only for sons of the same mother or was general but I incline to think that the same method would hold.

Another informant, who owned land in common with an elder brother of the same mother, told me that when they came to divide their land his elder brother would get land in the proportion of eight shares to his six. But before sharing land or anything else the eldest brother first gets two - whether pieces of land, breadfruit trees or what not.

Before leaving the question of the inheritance of ancestral land it is worth noting that here again the observer may be confused by hearing land referred to as belonging to such and such a woman. In extended family C for instance I was often told of any particular piece of land that it belonged to C^1 who was a widow with no son. The real meaning was that the land had been that of her husband. Neither he not any other male member of the land owning group was surviving and the land had been inherited by C^5, the nearest male kinsman. But during the lifetime of the original owner's widow, C^1, it was referred to as hers and she would farm on it. In the same way C^2, another widow with no son, was spoken of as owning land.

If a widow has a son who is still a child her husband's land will sometimes be referred to as hers until her son grows up. But this manner of speech does not in any way mean that women really own land.

IV NON-FREEBORN INHABITANTS OF UMUEKE AND THE LAND

a) OSU

There were in Umueke a fair number of OSU (.') - of people, that is to say, who had been bought and dedicated to one or other of the various deities in the village. These people, as in the many other parts of Ibo country where they are found, are a class apart in the sense that marriage or sexual intercourse between them and non-OSU people is strictly taboo.

So far as land is concerned one informant told me that if a man bought a male OSU he would hand him over to one of his wives to look after and he would help her with her farm work, Either then or later on the master of the OSU would show him part of his own land where he could farm. When the master married a wife for him the master's own wife would give the OSU's wife a bit of her own MGBALA (...) - garden. C^1 told me that if an extended family had a tract of common land - ALA OZUZU OHA [1] any OSU people they might own would be shown land there for farming each season. This, he said, was what happened in the case of the OSU A6, owned by extended family A. Whereas if an extended family had no ALA OZUZU OHA some of its members would apportion part of their land permanently to their OSU people.

As a matter of fact it is not invariable for an OSU to farm on ALA OZUZU OHA in cases where it exists. In 1937 I saw A^6 the OSU of extended family A, farming on a piece of land which A^3 had shown him for the season and which A^3 held personally. It was pledge land which he had inherited. But in any case the custom is that an OSU will be shown land for farming by the person or people who have bought him. If in the course of time he has many children or descendants and they need more land they will get it on pledge or get it 'shown' to them for a season just as other people do.

b) SLAVES - OHU ('.)

The same word, OHU, is used both for a bought slave and for a

---

1 See p.6.

pawn, the latter being a person who has pledged himself to someone else in return for a sum of money and is therefore bound, in most cases, to work for him and usually to live with him. Unlike wealthier places such as Owerri and Egbu where there are considerable numbers of OHU Umueke has few, if any, and I had no opportunity of seeing at first hand how they would obtain land. But C1 told me that an OHU would just be allowed by his master to plant his yams on the edge of where he himself was farming and would not be shown land by him for his permanent use.

I did not go into the question of whether slaves could obtain land on pledge or lease it from other people but I heard nothing to suggest that they could not.

c) STRANGERS

A man who has left his own town and wants to settle down in Umueke can approach one of the extended families for land.

C^8 was a stranger who had fled from his own place after some dispute and had come to Umueke. He had taken palm wine and gone to extended family C and had asked for land to farm on. They agreed to show him land each year for eight years. For the first five years a different one among them showed him land each year. They then told him he could plant on their ALA OZUZU OHA which he did for several years. After about ten years he 'bought' land of his own - that is to say he got some on pledge. The houses of himself and his wives were at a little distance from the housegroup of extended family C, who formed a compact settlement. I was told that he had been carefully cross examined by his hosts as to his intentions - whether he was really going to settle in Umueke and pay tax there and so on. And I know that he had sworn many oaths of mutual good-will with D^5. By now he is taken, I was told, as an Umueke man. I noticed that he took his place, being fairly old, at gatherings of the elders, but my impression was that his position was that of a junior rather than a senior member when it came to sharing palm wine.

V RIGHTS OVER TREES AND PERMANENT CROPS ON LAND OWNED IN COMMON BY A GROUP OF KINSMEN

a) OIL PALMS. In the village of Umueke there are no permanent cultivated economic crops of the type of cocoa or cotton planted or cultivated systematically for sale on a big scale.

There are a certain number of trees of commercial value such as iroko and there are many trees, more fully described later, whose fruit is used as food either for consumption or for sale in the local markets. The chief permanent economic crop is of course palm nuts. The palm trees - ŊKWƟ (˙˙) - are said normally to be self sown though I have been told that if a tree is seen to produce good and plentiful nuts some of them may be planted. But usually oil palms are uncultivated products of the bush.

Rights in the important matter of cutting palm nuts were in an interesting state of ambiguity in Umueke. During my stay there, first in 1935 and again in 1937, the pendulum swung uneasily between the restriction of rights to those who owned the land on which the palms stood and the extension of rights to anyone to cut anywhere. In outline the position was that whereas formerly people had been allowed to cut palm nuts on other people's land it had later been decided that they should cut only on their own or their father's land - that is to say that they should keep within the limits of their land owning group. This was the state of affairs during most of 1935, but towards the end of the year the position was challenged by the younger men who insisted that there should be a return to communal methods of cutting. When I got back in 1937 there was still disagreement, but in practice there seemed to be a compromise midway between the two extremes.

As the question is one of considerable interest it will perhaps be worth giving rather more in detail what one saw and heard. When I first got to the village early in 1935 I was told that D^5, the eldest man in the village, had been instrumental in getting a 'law' passed[1] to the effect that palm nuts should not be cut in common but only by those on whose land they stood. It was said that he had done this because he himself had many palm trees on his land. One also noticed that he was an elderly man whose climbing and cutting capacity would be less than that of a vigorous youth and that he had thus a double reason for wanting people to stick to their own land.

A little later, when talking to several men of the village, I was told that in past years anyone could cut anywhere. But, they said, it had been seen that the strongest people cut to the detriment of the less strong. So a new arrangement had been made and now people could only cut on their own land - that is to say within the land of the land owning group. Later one of these men and another informant said that rights had not been entirely communal formerly in the sense that people could cut anywhere in the whole of Umueke but that each man could cut in his own division of the village. That is to say that an Umueke-ama man could cut anywhere in Umueke-ama, an Umunwaebodim man anywhere in Umunwaebodim and an Umueke-owɛrɛ man anywhere in Umueke-owɛrɛ. These informants also added that it was the coming of tax that caused the swing over from relatively communal to private rights. Some people who were unable to climb saw others climbing the palms on their land and cutting the nuts, but when they asked these people to help them pay their tax they were refused, to their great vexation. So it was decided that a man should only cut palm nuts on his own land.

That restricted rights over palms had been in fact established was borne out by a case in September 1935 when a young man of Umunwaebodim was fined twenty ɔla (˙.) - about one and eight pence - by the village for cutting palm nuts on the land of another Umunbodim man. The accuser said he caught him in the act. He then referred to the 'law' which he said had been made early that year,

---

1 Regulations that the village made for itself are always referred to as IWU (.˙) - law - though they may or may not win their way to general acceptance.

that people should not cut palm nuts except on their own or their father's land. Before that palms had been owned in general but now they were private property and he demanded compensation, which the assembled villages awarded him, from the thief. Two other people were convicted at the same time and four others were accused.

Whether or not the Umunwaebodim man was accurate in saying that the rights of private ownership had only been so recently established as that year, the case none the less confirms the statements of informants recorded above that earlier communal ownership had been replaced by restricted rights.

But at the end of October I happened one morning to meet two young men of Umueke-owerɛ striding along with their matchets and saying that the law about palm trees had been changed in the direction of communal ownership and that they were going to cut any they saw. Overhearing this, A^6, the old OSU belonging to extended family A, came up to me in a state of great agitation and said that this would bring much palaver. That evening D^4, who was a strong headed and independent young man, came to my house after the eight day Umueke market looking very cook-a-hoop and said that he and his ƐBIRI (˙..) - age grade - had gone that afternoon in the market to the ƐBIRI of D^5 - that is to say of the elders of the village - and had made them alter the 'law' about cutting palm nuts. The young men had insisted that hence forward they should be cut 'in general', each man cutting where he liked. The only exceptions, were to be palm trees that were being tapped and ŊKWƏ ALƆ (˙˙˙.)[1]. D^4 said that D^5 had got two special places where palms were very plentiful and which he wanted to keep to himself and that he was angry at the new arrangement for communal cutting. But D^4 said that as his ƐBIRI was numerous they bore down the opposition of the elders. If the latter had refused to concede what they wanted they would have seized their cows and sheep and sold them, since they must live somehow. As he said, it is all very well for the old men, they have all got wives, but the young ones have still to get together bride price to marry theirs and they need palm oil to sell. On the other hand one of the angry elders was heard to complain that he and his like, who had wives, have to share the profit of the palm nuts with their wives, who get the kernels. Whereas, he said, the younger, unmarried men get oil, kernels and all.

Incidentally all this palm nut palaver was interesting in the light it threw on the way the village managed its affairs.But this is not the place to go into that aspect of the matter.

D^4 proceeded to explain to me how palm nuts had been cut in earlier days. His account differed in certain details from those already recorded, but confirmed their main outline.His version was that originally people used to cut nuts on their own land. Then came a time when people of Umueke were very few. Many died and only about thirty remained. This I had heard in another connection. When they were so few it was decied that all should cut where they liked throughout Umueke. They then begat children and became num-

---

1 See p.20

erous again and again decided that people should cut only on their own land. And it was this decision that D^4 and his ƐBIRI had forced the village to rescind in favour of communal cutting.

Shortly after this I went on leave, so had no opportunity of observing how far the new arrangement was really enforced. But when I returned more than a year later, in the beginning of 1937, an intermediate position between the extreme communalists and the extreme restrictionists seemed to have been reached. D^4 still told me that he had the right to cut nuts anywhere in Umueke or even in all Agbaja, though whether he tried to do so I do not know. I doubt it. But even D^8, who as the son of D^5 would have had every interest in supporting the contention that people might only cut on their own or their father's land, told me that an Umueke-ama man could cut anywhere in Umueke-ama. He would not, however, go outside this unless his house happened to be very near Umunwaebodim land and one of their palm trees was quite near his house. In that case he might cut it. Conversely, even within his own division of Umueke-ama, he would not go and cut from a palm just outside someone else's house. Abstract right, in fact, should be tempered by mutual forbearance and good manners. C^1 confirmed the general principle of D^8's statement independently by saying that any of the land-owning groups of extended family C could cut nuts on each other's land and could also cut, for instance, on the land of D^5. No one, however, would go to someone else's land and cut nuts from a palm that was being tapped for wine. From these two informants one sees that by 1937 there was a compromise between those who wanted people to cut anywhere and those who wanted people to cut only on their own land.

As to the influence exerted by tax in all these changes, opinions were contradictory. One informant in 1935 said, as we have seen, that tax caused the early phase of relatively communal ownership of palms to be superseded by the private ownership that existed in 1935 before the action of the young men. On the other hand another informant at the end of 1937 said that it was tax that had made people want the present right to cut anywhere.

What is evident however is that anything tending to increase the need for money - the introduction of tax, the increasing demand for European clothing, for schooling and so on, - would enhance the economic value for palms nuts and make a definition of rights a matter of importance. And in the process of definition divergence of interest could hardly fail to appear between those who had many palms on their land and those who had few. And a further dissension would arise between those who were young and strong and therefore wanted to cut where they liked and those who were weak and old and wanted to preserve their palms for themselves. The two lines of cleavage would not necessarily coincide. But where they did, as in Umeake and notably in the case of D^5, one got the formation of two opposing parties and a resulting compromise.

A further point to notice is that the question of rights over palm trees becomes a matter of real practical importance in the case of anyone wanting to plant the selected palm seedlings issued by the Agricultural Department. At the end of 1937 I took C^1 over the Government agricultural plantations at Umudike. He was greatly interested and was fired with a desire to try some seedlings himself. But he said the great difficulty would be to establish his exclusive right to them. He would not dare plant them anywhere but close to his house and even so it would, he seemed to think, be risky. He said that there would have to be a 'law' to prevent others from coming to cut palms a man had planted thus. I do not see why this should be difficult when one remembers that a man who has built a house on someone else's land[1] can claim ownership of any palms he has planted provided he has planted them in lines in the presence of witnesses.

All these changing rights as to palm trees concern men, since they and not women are the owners. But there is one case in which a woman can own palm trees and own them individually. When a women has born a child her husband, or his father if he is alive, will give her a palm tree at the foot of which the child's umbilical cord will be buried when it drops off several days after birth. The mother of the baby will henceforward have exclusive rights over the nuts of this tree. This at least is the rule. But, as with all Ibo rules, practice is apt to deviate. I have known a woman's mother-in-law lay claim to the nuts of these ƊKWƟ ALƆ - palm tree of the umbilical cord during her life time, on the understanding that her daughter-in- law would have them at her death. But in any case the rights over these nuts are exercised by an individual woman. When she dies the trees are inherited by her sons wives, the wife of the eldest getting the biggest share. And in Umeke this is the only case in which a woman owns palms in her own right and gets the money from the sale of the oil she makes. A widow with no son has the right to her husband's palm trees during her lifetime. But whether she would get the oil as well as the kernels or whether it would go to the man who cut for her I am not sure. I have seen a widow selling oil for herself but this may not always be the case. I noticed that where there were several widows of the same husband squabbles were apt to arise about the palm nuts.

In some other Ibo districts there are certain seasons in which women are allowed to have the palm nuts for their own profit. And women can own palm trees. But in Umeake this is not so. When I asked the Umueke men whether there was any season during which women would have the right to the palm nuts in the bush they laughed and said no, if once they let the women start having the palm nuts they would never leave off and they added that their palms are the men s only way of making money.

Palm oil is, as elsewhere, made by the joint labour of men and women but in Umueke the oil belongs to the man, who gets the money for which it is sold, The woman gets the money for the kernels.

In 1937 an oil press was introduced into Umueke and the owner, a stranger, charged sixpence on each tin of oil pressed. This sixpence was paid by the man who owned the nuts and not by his wife.

---

1 See p. 33

In Umueke and, as far as I know, elsewhere in Ibo country, it is forbidden for a woman to climb. She is therefore dependent on the man who cuts palm nuts for her and this constitutes one of his main claims to the oil. I used to wonder what would happen if the selected palms of the Agricultural Department were to be introduced into the village. They bear after a few years growth and, at first anyway, at a height where the bangas can easily be cut without climbing. If women were to plant and cut such trees themselves it is interesting to speculate as to what would happen to the balance of ownership between men and women in the matter of palm nuts.

b) Rights over tapping oil palm trees for palm wine.

In Umueke palm wine is chiefly obtained by tapping the oil palm NKWΘ (˙˙) - and not the wine palm ŊGWƆ (˙.) - the latter being scarce. The right to tap is more circumscribed than the right to cut palm nuts as only certain trees produce wine well. It will be stated that a man can tap any palm in the land of his own division of the village - i.e. an Umueke-ama man can tap anywhere in Umueke-ama provided no one else has already started tapping the tree. But at the same time, when land is shared up between its several owners, palm trees for tapping will be divided separately according to the number of trees and not according to the plot of land they grow on. The man taking chief share of the land will take two palms for himself and will then share them on the basis of getting two more than the next sharer.

c) Trees whose produce is used and to which rights of ownership are attached.

There are a number of trees whose produce - fruit, leaves, etc - is used for food and other purposes and over which definite rights of ownership are recognised. In many cases the trees are planted. Among the most important of such trees are the wine palm - ŊGWƆ (˙.); bread fruit - ΘKWA (˙.); oilbean - ΘGBAKALA (.˙..); native pear - UBƐ (.˙); ƆHA(.˙); banana - UNƐRƐ; cocoa-nut - AKΘBƐKƐ (˙˙_). The general principle governing rights over such trees is that the joint owners of the land on which they stand own their produce in common. Whether or not an individual among them who plants a tree on this land owns its produce separately I am not sure but I rather think so[1].

When the time comes for the land to be divided up between the various owners the trees owned in common will be divided separately tree by tree. They will not simply pass with the land. The senior member of the land owning group will get the largest number according to the usual rules of inheritance. If the members are brothers of the same mother D[4] said that the eldest brother would, in the case of each kind of tree, get two more than the next brother and at least in the case of some trees he would start by getting two for himself in addition to this.

I came across one case where reincarnation affected minor rights

---

[1] The planting of trees confers certain rights of individual ownership in some cases. See p.p. 22, 33.

of inheritance. A baby was born in Umunwaebodim who was said to be the reincarnation of a deceased kinsman who had died childless. This baby, it was said, would inherit the bread-fruit and other trees that the dead man had planted.

I add a few notes about certain of the trees listed above:-

WINE PALM. Not much used for wine in Umueke but the leaves are important in roofmaking. The property of men.

COCOA NUT
NATIVE PEAR } The fruit of both belongs usually to men.

BREADFRUIT. There is a specially proprietary feeling about these trees since they are planted deliverately. Their fruit is looked on as a woman's perquisite and will belong to the wives of the men who own the trees. In Umueke this fruit is quite an important food and is also taken to market and sold for local consumption. There is a special way of mashing it that is the monopoly of the women of certain places since they only know how to do it. It is therefore a source of gain to them.

One man told me that if he and his brother, who was of the same mother, held land in common between them, when they had both married wives they would probably divide their bread fruit trees even though the land remained undivided, so that palaver between the wives would be avoided. As he put it, one wife will get up earlier than the others and take more than her share of fruit and then there will be rows. So it is better to divide the trees. One certainly often sees a bread fruit lying on the ground with a piece of twig stuck in it. This means that someone has found it and lays claim to it and cannot carry it away just then so has put it under supernatural protection to prevent anyone else from taking it. This serves to show that importance is attached to breadfruit in Agbaja though in places like Owerri where yams and food generally are more plentiful this would probably not be so.

When a man dies, if he has no son his widow will have the right to his breadfruit during her life time. If he has a son he will divide the produce of the breadfruit trees between his mother and his own wives, the former getting the largest share.

A woman may plant breadfruit trees of her own, in which case the trees belong to her with their produce. When she dies they will be inherited by her son's wives, the wife of the eldest son getting first share.

OILBEAN. The rights over these trees are rather less definite than over breadfruit. They seem to be looked on as less important. It was said that an oilbean tree with very little fruit on it would be cut by anyone. But if the beans were enough to fill two baskets, only the owner might cut them. One man said also that children would cut oilbean whenever they saw it. All the same oil bean trees are, as we have seen, reckoned as property by the people on whose land they are. How far the beans belong to men and how far to women is again less clear than in the case of breadfruit. One man told me that the fruit of oilbean trees on a man's land is the property of a man. Another said that if he had, say, four oilbean trees ae would keep the fruit of one to be sold for his own profit but would let his wives have the fruit of the others to use for food or for sale. A woman may plant oilbean trees of her own which will be owned and inherited in the same manner as are breadfruit.

A considerable amount of oilbean is used as a form of 'kola' in entertaining strangers and for snacks in between meals. Small packets of sliced oilbean are sold by women in large quantities in the local markets. The unsliced beans are also sold.

OHA. The leaves of this tree are much used for making soup and are looked on as a woman's perquisite. Wives will have the OHA leaves of their husband's trees.

The OHA tree is often planted as part of the shrine for a person's CI, - his creating spirit. When land is divided among its co-owners the ordinary OHA trees are divided among them according to the number of trees, as in the usual procedure. But the OHA CI, the OHA which are CI shrines, are left as common property of the people who originally owned the land, and their wives share the leaves among them. For instance in Umueke the large extended family of Umunwaebodim have in common the OHA CI of the 'mother who bore them all', one Lolo Dimamako, the wife of their common ancester Dimamako, the father of the Nwaebodim, from whom they take their name. Its leaves, as I witnessed, are shared among all the married women of Umunwaebodim. Towards the end of the wet season they come together and share the leaves and each contribute a small sum of money. With this money a fowl is bought which is sacrificed by the senior man of Umunwaebodim at this OHA CI on the day the women do their annual religious rites.

BANANA. Banana fruit is looked on as belonging to women. A woman will also plant and own trees. One sees palaver ensuing if any woman cuts the fruit of another woman's tree

ORANGES. I saw no sweet oranges growing in Umueke. The few that grew in the next door village were man's property not woman's. But they had little or no commercial value since there was no European demand within marketable distance.

FIREWOOD. Firewood must not be cut on the cultivated land of anyone else. But it can be cut on land belonging to anyone of the same division of the village - e.g. Umueke-ama - as the cutter.

V PLEDGING LAND

Land can be, and frequently is, pledged by the owner to another person in return for a sum of money. The owner can redeem it at any time by repayment of the original sum, the produce of the land being looked on as the interest on the money.

In Umueke life was on a modest scale and I only came on fairly small scale transactions involving amounts of about fifteen shillings to a pound. I saw for instance one bit of land of perhaps a couple of acres that had been pledged some years previously for one pound.

As we noticed elsewhere, it is important not to be led into misconceptions by the Ibo words used in a pledging transaction. There is the quite unambigious expression EGBA IBƐ (˙···) - to pledge. But one also repeatedly hears that land has been 'bought', the Ibo word used being EZΘ (˙·) - to buy - this being the word used for buying such things as goats, food or clothes, But when used of land it is merely a figure of speech. If you say to the speaker: 'Do you really mean that that land has been bought outright?' he will decisively say no and will proceed to point out that in no circumstances can land be bought or sold outright. Land cannot be 'lost' is the saying. And when the man who has pledged land brings the original sum of money, the individual to whom he has pledged it cannot refuse to take the money and part with the land, If he tries to do so the other will call the elders together and they will give decision in his favour saying: 'Can land be lost thus?'.

This does not mean that the original owner of the land can seize it back at any moment regardless of time and season. If his 'tenant' had got a yam or coco yam crop in the ground the landowner would have to wait till the crop had been dug. He would also wait if cassava had been newly planted. But if a grown cassava crop were standing in the land he would tell the 'tenant that his wife must dig up the cassava and if she failed to do so he would do so himself and then resume the land. The 'tenant' is thus protected against sudden or unreasonable eviction. In Mbieri the village group of my interpreter, I was told that the owner would ordinarily go and demand his land back in December or January, after the main harvest and before other crops are likely to have been planted.

One informant told me that if, as is normally the case, there are a number of relatives owning land in common, anyone of them wanting to pledge a piece of the land ought, according to right custom, to consult the others before doing so. If they agree, the one wanting to pledge goes ahead and the money he receives is his own individual property. It is not shared with his co-landowners. They will tell him that he should redeem the land in six months ; but if this is so, and I only heard it from this one informant, I cannot help feeling that this is more in the nature of a pious hope than of a serious expectation. Land sometimes remains pledged not only for years but for generations. In any case if, in the course of time, these co-landowners decide to divide the land up between them, either as individuals or as smaller groups, the land which this one of their number originally pledged and failed to redeem will be counted as part of his share. It will sometimes happen that a man needs money urgently and if his co-landowners are not available he will pledge a piece of land without consulting them. But this is not really correct procedure.

Another informant, C^1, who happened to be the eldest of three brothers of the same mother, all owning land in common, told me that if he wanted to pledge a piece of the ancestral land he would consult his brothers first if he was on good terms with them, but not otherwise. They however could not pledge land without consulting him. He is not under any real necessity to ask their consent, though I gathered, without being quite sure of the point, that if they chose to make a fuss about it they could complain to the elders. They would not be likely to do so unless a quarrel arose. But if one brother pledges land the others will expect him to redeem it in due course and another informant, who was a younger brother, told me that there would be palaver between himself and his eldest brother if the latter did not redeem some land he had pledged for a pound when he was marrying a wife.

The person who is paying money in exchange for pledged land will take care that he had witnesses to the transaction. He will also make sure that the co-landowners of the man who is pledging land know what is happening, as he does not want them later to repudiate the bargain.

Land which X has obtained on pledge from Y or has inherited from the man who originally obtained it from Y he can repledge at will. One informant apparently held that this could be done as a normal procedure. Another said that if X wanted his money back he ought first to go to Y, the landowner, and ask if he would redeem it. If Y did not want to do so he would tell X to repledge the land to Z. Then when Y wanted the land back he would give the money to X who would give it to Z. But if X repledged to Z without consulting Y, Y would be angry. Also X should not repledge for more than the original sum he paid.

I have not come across a case in Umueke of a dispute about land repledged for more than the original sum, though it may of course happen. But in Mbieri such disputes arise.

As we have seen earlier, no form of outright sale of land is recognised by native law and custom. This cannot be too strongly emphasised nor too fully grasped by anyone who has dealings with the Ibo. But here, as in other societies, the law tends to lag behind practical social requirements and modifications are made in fact if not in theory. An interesting example of such adjustment arises in the case of land pledging. In theory land cannot be permanently alienated by sale. But there are certain cases in which an individual may want to aquire a certain piece of land with the reasonable certainty of being able to keep it. It may just round off some property of his own or be in some particularly convenient position for him. It is therefore worth rather more to him than its current pledge value and he will get it on pledge in return for a larger sum of money than would be offered by someone wanting it temporarily. This in no way prejudices the right of the owner to redeem it at anytime but it means that he is very unlikely to do so. For instance, as one informant pointed out, he may have received two pounds in return for pledging a piece of land whose normal exchange value is one pound ten shillings. When therefore, if ever, the time comes that he wants more land he will not take two pounds and redeem his original land but will take one pound ten shillings and get an equivalent piece of pledge from someone else.

I first heard of this type of transaction in Owerri town[1], where I was told of it by a sophisticated informant who quite realised its implications - that it practically means permanent occupation of the land. I do not know how often it occurs in Owerri. In Umueke I only came on one case of it though there may have been others. I have no idea whether or not there is much of this type of pledging in Ibo country but I record it as an interesting practical way of getting round the prohibition of the sale of land. But the fact that legally the land is not alienated and can, at need, still be redeemed is an important safeguard,

One could not but feel the need for some such safeguard in observing this whole question of the pledging of land. One saw the lighthearted way in which young men would pledge land they did not need at the moment. D^4 pointed out to me how reckless D^1 and D^2 were being in this way. They were young men going away at intervals to work and they had as yet practically no yams. They had pledged six pieces of their land and D^4, who was of the same land owning group, was protesting at their wishing to use still more land for farming.

In such a case one saw how easily, if the sale were allowed, a young man would part with his land for the irresistable temptation of ready cash, without any thought for the future. While he can only pledge it he can at least repent at leisure and redeem it, or his family for him, when work fails or when he wants to marry and settle down.

The inheritance of ancestral land is different from that of land held on pledge,[2] The latter is reckoned in with a man's personal property and is inherited by his heirs after his death as are his money, goats, yams and other personal possessions. One of the things that a father during his lifetime will be specially careful about is to

---

1 I use the word 'town' rather than 'village group' for Owerri because such is the general usage. Also Owerri is sufficiently compact and urban to make 'town' as suitable a word as 'village group',

2 When one speaks of the inheritance of land held on pledge one means of course inheritance of the right to hold the land till it is redeemed and when it is redeemed to receive the money for it.

show his son any pieces of land that he holds on pledge. And whereas it seemed that in the case of ancestral land inheritance was likely more or less to follow customary lines,[1] I was told by D^4 that with personal property the individual wishes of the owner may modify customary rules. How far in fact this is the case I had no opportunity of observing but I give D^4's statement as he gave it to me. He explained that if one son has been specially attentive to his father in such matters as fetching him firewood or working for him on days other than ORIƐ (..), which is the customary day, and if the father thus specially loves him, he will leave him extra bits of his property when he dies. He can give him anything he likes. While he is alive he may call the boy and show him where he keeps his money - my informant accompanied these remarks by dramatic gestures - and tell him when he dies to comes and take it and the others will not know. Or he may tell his debtors that when he dies this is the son to whom they are to repay debts. He also said that the father might leave property to anyone, other than his sons, who had been good to him. Such a one would probably be a near kinsman.

I asked A^3 who would be the heir of such a man as his father's younger brother who had died leaving no son. He replied that it would be anyone who had run messages for him and helped him in his lifetime and that in this case it was himself. He explained that when his father's brother died his kinsfolk went to a dibea (·.) - diviner - and asked him who should be the heir of the dead man and who should do his second burial. As a result of this consultation A^3, who was a young man did the second burial in the sense of providing the customary goat and fowl. Then when it came to his inheriting the dead man's property A^3's brothers disputed his right. So he called the elders of Umueke and asked them to judge the case. And they, hearing that it was only A^3 who had contributed to the second burial, decided that he was the rightful heir. And among other things he inherited land which his father's brother had held on pledge. This he now held individually apart from the ancestral land that he and his brothers owned in common. But though land held on pledge is really of the nature of private property and is not the affair of the holder's land owning group, difficulties may arise if the holder dies leaving no grown up son. The widows of D^6 used to complain bitterly to me that the kinsmen of their husband were seizing and using the lands he had obtained on pledge and the fruit trees he had planted, instead of leaving them for his small sons. This case may have neem exceptional however. The widows were from distant Aro cuku and could not summon their relatives to support them or the case would probably have been tried in the village. Even D^8, the son of the chief culprit, admitted that the lands D^6 had had on pledge where the affair of his eldest small son. He was indignant with D^3 and D^4, who were of the same extended family as himself and D^6 but of a different land owning group. They had pledged land to D^6 and after his death D^8 found that they had, without further ceremony, repledged it to another man. They ought of course to have redeemed the land by repaying to D^6's small son whatever D^6 had originally paid for it. They ought then to have informed D^5, the senior kinsman of the dead man.

---

1 See p.12

A person who has obtained land on pledge has no right over the fruit of trees, whether palms or other, on that land unless he has made a special arrangement with the owner to this effect. The owner may, for extra payment, grant him rights over the fruit of the trees but this will not include the right to cut them down. Conversely trees such as bread fruit or oilbean may be pledged quite apart from land.

As to the rights of the pledge tenant - the man who has obtained land on pledge- over trees he himself plants in the land while he holds it, I give the views of several different men informants. One Umueke man, C1,told me that if a pledge tenant planted such trees as bread fruit, pear, kola, in the land he held, these trees would continue to belong to him when the land was redeemed by its owner and he would have the right to their fruit. I gathered that he couldnot however cut them down. I was not quite clear as to whether the land owner was also allowed to pick part of the crop, but I fancy this was not my informant's meaning. What he did say after giving this information was that anyone can plant fruit trees in another person's land, without holding it on pledge, provided he gets the permission of the land owner. He said, in fact, that this planting can be done and the land owner informed afterwards and he will not mind. The planter will come and pick the fruit of the trees for himself. But he will al so allow the land owner to pick and keep a part. It isyams and coco yams, said my informant, over which the land owner whoplants them has exclusive rights.

Having in mind disputes which have arisen west of the Nigerabout cocoa crops planted, so far as I remember, on pledged land, I asked my informant what would happen if he himself gave land on pledge to another man and that man planted so many fruit trees in it for the purpose of selling their fruit that when he himself redeemed theland there would be no room in it for him to plant yams or coco yam. He said that if he saw his pledge tenant planting many fruit trees - I could not use cocoa as an example as it is not grown in this area - he would tell him to stop and if he refused he himself would cut them down. The tenant ought not to plant more than four or five fruittrees in any one plot of ground. Such a plot would probably be quite small-perhaps an acre or less. Another Umueke man whom I asked about the same matter of rights over trees planted on pledged land replied rather differently. He said that if the pledge tenant plants fruit trees, when the owner of the land redeems it he will 'drag' with the tenant about the trees saying did he ask him to plant trees in his land? And he will try to claim possession of them. To which my Mbieri interpreter remarked that the fact of his 'dragging' really means that he realises the trees belong to the planter. But this Umueke informant, like the other, at once went on to the subject of planting fruit trees on another person's land rather than on land held on pledge, as though this were a more normal and safe procedure. He said that anyone could ask permission to plant fruit trees in another man's bush and he, the planter, would then own these trees.

I cannot remember seeing a case of fruit trees planted by a tenant on the land he held on pledge though I have seen cases of tenants who have acquired rights over trees already there in the land they held on pledge.

But my Mbieri interpreter spoke emphatically about the situation in his more advanced village group of Mbieri. He said that there if a pledge tenant planted fruit trees in the land he held on pledge he would continue to own the trees and their fruit after the land had been redeemed. I cited the case of cocoa and asked what would happen if the pledge tenant planted a crop like this. He admitted that it was a difficult case, because the owner of the land, when he redeemed it, would not have room to plant yams or coco yams. But he said that even so he thought that in his town the cocoa would belong to the man who had planted it and would not revert to the land owner with the land. It was however, to him, a hypothetical case, since no such situation had, so far as I know, ever arisen in his own place. Nor have I myself come across any such in Ibo country.

It is clear I think, from the above, that the exact rights over permanent crops on pledged land are not yet fully defined, since the need for such definition has not yet arisen. There are however, indications in present custom as to the lines on which future decisions may emerge.

VI LETTING OR 'SHOWING' LAND FOR A SEASON FOR FARMING

Land obtained on pledge may be kept for an indefinite period - until such time, in fact as the owner wishes to redeem it. And the widespread custom of pledging is undoubtedly a factor making for flexibility in the land situation. That is to say that it is a means by which surplus land can be temporarily transferred to someone other than the owner, who needs the use of it. This is important in such a thickly populated area.

But there is another and equally widespread custom which, for lack of a better word, may be called the short term leasing of land, provided that one defines clearly what such 'leasehold' tenure means in native law and custom. This further factor making for flexibility and, in some parts of Ibo country, for the commercialisation of land, needs stressing as it is sometimes unknown in European circles.

The Ibo word for this short term letting of land is IZI (˙·) or in some dialects IZHI (˙·) - to show. This same word is used in certain special cases of land made over permanently to another person as is sometimes done when a man buys an OSU[1] and showshim certain bits of land where he can farm regularly. But the ordinary meaning, if a man says of another 'I have shown him some land' is that he has given the man who thus becomes his tenant permission to plant crops such as yam - JI (˙) or coco yam - ƐDƐ (˙.), or cassava - JI APƟ (˙˙·), for one season.

The procedure of this 'showing' tenure for a season is as follows. A man who wants some land other than his own on which to farm will take palm wine and go to the owner of the ground he wants and ask if he will 'show' him some land on which he can cut bush and

---

1 See p.15

farm for one season. If a man of Umueke shows land thus to another Umueke man or to any other Agbaja man the tenant will not pay any money. But at the end of the farming season, according to C^1, he will take more palm wine to the land owner and a basket of pounded food and about two shilling's worth of dried fish. The land owner will call his extended family to share this food. And he will also cook food and about six pennyworth of fish for his tenant.

But if an Umueke man 'shows' land for a farming season to a non-Agbaja tenant, the tenant, at the end of the season, when he has dug his yams, will, according to one informant, bring three shillings rent to the landowner, or four or five shillings if he is not a friend of his. D^4 told me that a non-Agbaja tenant would give palm wine for the land and about twenty yams when he dug his crop. But he did not mention money in transaction. When a landowner 'shows' land to a tenant thus he does not bargain about the size of the land. The tenant just takes as such as he has yams for. There is little fear of the tenant seizing more land than he needs as he certainly will not trouble to clear bush in excess of what he wants for his crops.

I could find no unit of measurement of land in Umueke such as there is of course, in Owerri and Mbieri. The only word one heard was ƆRƟ (˙˙), which simply meant a farm of what ever size, This is a further indication, I think, that land conditions in Agbaja, though fairly flexible owing to the pressure of population, have not yet gone far towards actual monetary commercialisation.

I was told that in Umueke there is no magico-religious ritual accompanying the 'showing' of land to a tenant.

People get others to 'show' them land thus for a farming season for a variety of reasons. Obviously if they have not enough land of their own or if what they have is poor they will try to lease land in this way. Or other considerations may come in. Aman I knew in Umueke-ama, who had plenty of good land of his own, went off one farming season to the neighbouring village of Abose Agbaja to farm. Having no wife to plant cassava for him he wanted to plant some for himself as well as yams. He knew that in Umueke cassava was liable to be decimated by goats and cows, who were only tied up during the yam season. He therefore went to Abose where he had a sister married and got his sister's husband to 'show' him land, because in Abose goats were better tied and the people did not keep cows. They did not like the latter. This livestock question, which was a constant irritant to the cropowners, often decided people of a densely populated village to plant cassava in a neighbouring and relatively sparse area, where it was possible to find land far away from the houses and their animals.

The Mbieri people, a large village group near Owerri, who are both wealthier and more sophisticated than the people of Agbaja and who are fairly densely populated, have rather different arrangements from Agbaja in their short term leasing of land for farming. Both here and in Owerri there is a recognised unit of land, called UBI (˙.) - farm - which, though it is not of a definite, uniform size, does none the less act as some sort of measure. The breadth is normally five rows of yams. And though the length is not definitely specified it has some recognised relation to the breadth, since an UBI that was very short would have to be of double breadth and contain ten rows of yams instead of five.

Whether an Mbieri man is leasing land for a farming season - one year in the case of yam or two for cassava - to a stranger or a co-townsman or even a co-villager, he will both charge a money rent and charge it in proportion to the amount of land leased. The rent will be about a shilling an UBI. But brothers of the same father will not take money from each other for land. And for a friend the rent will be halved or even abrogated. Where no rent is charged the tenant will give palm wine to the land owner at the beginning of the season. But the tenant will not cook food for the owner at the end of the season. And though he may give him yams there is no obligation either of law or of custom to do so. Nor will the owner necessarily take them. But the tenant will acquire kudos if he gives a good number of yams. People will say he has AKA IKE (`...) - strong hand.

With a few old people the custom still persists by which the tenant, when he is going to start farming, will take palm wine to the land owner, who, after drinking, will pour some on the ground and call on ALA (..) - the ground[1]- to make the land produce well for the tenant[2].

In Onitsha, where there is a large urban population, I gathered that land was being impoverished by over farming and that fire wood was becoming scarce. Here, as at Nkwelle nearby, land which would formerly have lain fallow for a number of years was being over-cultivated because of the rent which could be got from it. Or in Onitsha labour would be hired to work land which formerly would have been left alone.

Land is leased both in Onitsha and in Nkwelle, where Onitsha goes to farm, for five shillings for a farming season whereas formerly payment would have been in yams. My informant, when I asked him how much land would be leased for this sum of money, said at first that the tenant would take as much as he wanted, as he would not take more than he could work, But he added that some people measure the land they lease and if the tenant wants more he must pay more than five shillings. The commercialisation of land is evident here both in the change to a money payment and in the measurement of the land leased.

---

1 Ala (..) - the earth - is a deity to all Ibo people. In Umueke there was an ALA shrine for the village, though no priest as there is in some places. But ALA is frequently invoked in prayers and sacrifices.

2 The above notes about Mbieri were given me by my Mbieri interpreter. Though I increasingly spoke and understood Ibo I also often, to a greater or lesser degree, used an interpreter.

At Ogbunike, twelve miles from Onitsha, towards the densely populated country round Awka, land is leased for a farming season for a money payment which varies from about five shillings to two shillings, outsiders being charged more than fellow townsmen. I did not hear of land being limited in amount for this payment. Where it is not limited the supposition presumably is that the tenant will only take what he requires for his immediate use.

The neighbouring town of Umudioka, which is short of land, goes and farms at Nkwelle where land is leased for money according to the size of the plot.[1]

VII 'SHOWING' LAND FOR HOUSEBUILDING

An individual may not only ask another man to 'show' him land for a season's farming, he may also ask for land on which to build a house.

A man who, because his family is troubled by sickness or for some other reason, decides to move his dwelling place, may be told by a DIBEA - diviner - to choose a site on someone else's land. He will take palm wine and go to the owner of the land and ask if he may build houses for himself and his people on it. If the owner is not on good terms with him he may at first refuse. But, as my informant put it, his people will beg him and will say: 'Does a person ever refuse land to someone who wants to build a house'? And eventually he will agree to grant the land. The housebuilder will occupy it for as long as he wants but when he no longer wishes to live there the land will revert to the owner. I have sometimes met the idea among Europeans that such land never reverts as the housebuilder would not vacate his house. This however ignores that fact that people quite often, for sickness and other reasons, do change their dwelling place. I have known several such cases, though the people do not of course necessarily move on to someone else's land. They may go to a different part of their own. But I have known a case in which a man has built on someone's else's land and eventually moved off it, the landowner resuming the land. The discussion below, therefore, of rights over trees planted by a housebuilder who has abandoned his site, is not purely academic. It has practical application.

When a man has been shown land by another on which to build a house he may cook a fowl and eat it with the owner of the land. This is not a sacrifice. But, if the DIBEA so directs, sacrifice may be made. The housebuilder will take a fowl and call the owner of the land to come and kill it. The latter will do so and will pray that the land may not kill or harm the housebuilder or his family. The formula used is: - ALA ƐMƐƐNA YA NHƐLI (..˙......) - Let not the land cause him to get up - i.e. Let not the land cause his people to die and hence cause him to get up and go elsewhere. If the housebuilder - the tenant - plants pear trees or kola or breadfruit or oil bean trees on the land these trees will continue to belong to him if

---

[1] The above notes about Onitsha, Nkwelle and Ogbunike were made during a short stay in the neighbourhood.

he afterwards goes to live elsewhere and the land itself reverts to the real owner. He, the planter, will come and pick their fruit in its season. He will give a small share of such things as pear and kola to the landowner but will take all the breadfruit for himself.He has the right to cut down the trees when he likes but would give the landowner a share of the wood of certain trees, breadfruit among them. If a tree ceased to bear fruit the landowner could cut it down but would, in the case of certain trres, give the planter a share of the wood.

If the tenant during his time of occupation plants oil palms in the presence of witnesses and in lines, he will continue to own them after the land has reverted to the original owner. But if he just plants them anyhow and without witnesses he will not be allowed to own them since palm trees are so common that no one will believe he planted them.

If the tenant's wife had planted banana and plantain while they were living on the land she would have the right to the crops in perpetuity after theland had reverted to the original owner. The fact that this fruit is an annual crop in the sense that each shoot only produces for one year and is then cut down does not invalidate the position. New shoots spring up each year and the original planter has the right to their crops. I was told that if, from this habit of annual new shoots, two people's banana or plantain clumps eventually merge, ownership of particular shoots will be carefully disentangled. One is struck repeatedly by the keenly developed Ibo sense of property.

VIII WOMEN AND THE USE OF THE LAND

Women do not, as we have seen, own land. But in Umueke they own much of its produce and play an even larger part than men in its cultivation. And a wife has definite customary rights to farm on her husband's land. Any description, therefore, of land tenure and the use of land would be unreal which did not take this into account. I therefore add a short note on this aspect of the use of the land.

As we have already seen, the women born in the village marry outside it. It is not, therefore, these daughters of the village who use its land but the women from elsewhere who marry into it. When a girl marries and comes to live with her husband, he, or his father if he is alive, will show her a piece of ground for her MGBALA - garden, - where she can plant her corn and vegetables among her busband's yams. This garden, being near the house, will be cultivated year after year since refuse is used to manure the ground.

The husband will also show his wife each year the farms that he is planting with yams that season so that she can plant more corn and vegetables there and probably also some coco yams and cassava. She will then keep the farm weeded. If she needs more land for her coco yam and cassava her husband or his father will show her land for that season. They will do the same if she has yams to pàant.

When a girl marries it is customary for her mother to give her coco yam and her father yam. In Umueke the yams will probably not be very many. Women are not big yam owners as they are in Owerri. The husband will not pay the last instalment of the bride price till he sees how many yams and coco yams the girls parents produce and if they do not come down handsomely he will probably pay no more at all. The occasions for haggling are of course almost unlimited.

These seed crops given the girl by her parents start her off in her farming at her husband's place. Cassava can of course be got by anyone since only the sticks and not the root are planted.

When her husband marries a second wife, the first one will give her a share of her garden to plant. They will each give the next wife a share and so on with subsequent wives. And the husband will each year, when he makes his farms, show each wife a piece of each farm in which to plant her crops among his yams. He will not, supposing he has three farms, let each wife plant in a different farm. All three will have a section of each farm. Any wife who needs it will also be given ground for the season for her yams or coco yams or cassava.

When a woman's son grows up her husband may allow him to plant his yams where his mother is planting her crops such as corn and vegetables. When the son marries it is customary that he should let both his wife and his mother plant in his farm among his yams.

It is possible for a man to give his wife a piece of ground for her permanent use if he cannot afford to give her the customary present of cloths, beads and so on known as IHE EGHOGHO AHO (˙˙..˙..)- things for washing body - when she comes finally to live with him. This present should be to the value of about one pound.

When a woman's husband dies she will go on planting in her MGBALA and her son will plant his yams there. She can also go on farming where she used to farm while her husband was alive.

Such is the general theme. One cannot go into the numerous variations here. But as an example one might note in passing that D^5, an old man with four living wives, had transferred his affections to the most recent of them and would let none of the others plant in his farms. They managed as best they could. One had several sons. Another had more than one lover. But it was not a peaceful family circle.

Farm work is shared between husband and wife with the children helping considerably. There is also co-operation between a mother and her grown up sons. And a man who has neither wife nor mother may have a lover who will help him in his farm work. C^5 managed thus. The woman did not plant her own crops among his yams as a wife would have done but she weeded for him and he in return gave her some yams when the time came to gig them.

The man's eaviest work is early in the season with the bush cutting and hoeing both for his own crops and those of his wife. Later on he puts sticks for the yams and trains their tendrils round them. After this he reckons his farm work finished till the time for digging yams. For the woman on the other hand farm work goes on all through the year.

In a place like Umueke-Agbaja where people have neither enough land nor enough money to warrant the hiring of labour as in Owerri - on the contrary the young men of Umueke and some of the girls go away to do farm work each year in the south where there is a demand for labour - the woman helps both with bush cutting and hoeing. The planting of the crops, both her own and her husband s, is her work and to her falls the recurrent work of weeding. She helps dig the harvest. And even after this, in the dry season, she may have crops like cassava or pepper to deal with. For her, farming is less intermittent than for the man.

Though cultivation is a co-operative affair between husband and wife they own their crops separately. And it is the woman who is expected to feed the family out of her own crops. Her husband may supplement her efferts in case of need. And if there are guests to entertain he may bring out some of his own yams to be cooked for them and will, now and then, give a few also to his own family. The rest he may sell. And it is the man of the family who provides meat on the rare occasions on which it is eaten. He also provides palm wine, that essential element of Ibo diet, and though it is he who mainly consumes it or uses it for hospitality, the women and children also get a share.

But the staple family food is provided by the woman. It does not include much yam. In a relatively poor community such as Agbaja yam is too expensive a luxury to be eaten in any great quantity. To the astonishment of my Owerri staff we found that in Umueke a woman would be looked on as extravagant who made ƟTARA(˙ . .)- pounded food, - of yam alone, without mixing coco yam or cassava with it.

In fact coco yam, cassava and bananas usually form the piece de resistence of the meat and are provided by the woman, either from her own farm or bought in the market. The soup which is the necessary relish to the meal is also made of ingredients provided by the woman.

This is the general outline. Again it would be possible to quote numbers of variations, such as an elderly man in Umunwaebodim who used to buy garri - grated cassava -and keep it in reserve at home to give his small children in case their mothers returned late from market and they were hungry. But in general it is admitted that it is the woman who feeds the family. This, combined with the fact that it is she who does the cooking, is incidentally a considerable source of quiet strength to her. If she is displeased with her husband go short of food. The couple who lived next door to me, D[8] and his wife, had a constant bone of contention in the shape of D 's lover whom his wife heartily disliked and whom he refused to abandon. When feeling was running high he would be apt to find no evening meal awaiting him at home and quite possibly no breakfast the next morning. And on more than one occasion the women of all Agbaja have, I was told, walked out on their husbands when their collective wrath was roused and stayed away till hunger and discomfort reduced the men to submission.

A further consequence of the woman's responsibility in the matter of food is her feeling of outrage when cows or other animals destroy her crops. Cows, goats and sheep are usually, though not invariably, the property of men, a woman more usually having a few fowls and perhaps a dog. The grievance about livestock eating the crops, which never seemed for long in abeyance and at times took on serious proportions, tended therefore to be a grievance of the women against the men. There were regulations about tying animals during the yam growing season but once that was over they were free to work their will on the cassava crop which, though now one of the chief foods, is of relatively recent introduction in any quantity and is unprotected by traditional rights.[1]

IX SUMMARY OF SALIENT POINTS WITH REGARD TO LAND TENURE IN UMUEKE AGBAJA

It may perhaps be useful to summarise very shortly some of the main points that have emerged from the foregoing description of land tenure in Umueke Agbaja.

i) Ownership of the land is broken up among small groups of kinsmen instead of being vested in large groups as is usually supposed to happen in primitive societies. An extended family containing five or six adult males and all living in one house group may be broken up into three different landowning groups though it may still also possess a tract of land in common.

All land is owned. It does not just lie about unclaimed as it presumably might in countries where population is sparse.

ii) There was nothing to suggest that any power over the land is vested in a 'chief' as it is in some parts of Africa. And the absence of this chiefly attribute and the dispersal of rights over the land among many small groups, accord with, and emphasise, the uncentralised and unauthoritarian nature of Ibo society.

iii) A marked feature of the land situation is its flexibility, by which is meant the ease with which land passes temporarily from hand to hand. It does not change ownership but it can be, and frequently is, obtained on a short term lease for a farming season or on pledge for an unspecified period. This is clearly of importance in easing the pressure on land of densely populated areas in those cases where more sparsely populated areas are near by. This ease in the temporary transference of land is of course one stage towards its commercialisation which has, in some areas of Ibo country, already been reached.

iv) It cannot however be too strongly emphasised that though rights over the use of land are transferable and though its ownership is in the hands of small rather than large groups and therefore seems to approximate to individual ownership, yet the sale of land is strongly forbidden by native law and custom.

---

1 One felt that the whole question of cassava needed investigating. From the point of view of diet it would appear to be considerably on the increase. If its food value is as poor and its effects as toxic as some expects seem to think, this can hardly be considered satisfactory.

One sometimes hears Europeans saying that land seems so nearly to be individually owned that the sale of land is surely the next logical step and can almost be assumed to have arrived. To the Ibo no such logic is apparent and he repeatedly repudiates the idea that land can be sold outright. This does not mean of course that if the sale of land were legalised land would not be sold. Ready money would be an irresistible temptation. This makes it all the more imperitive to weigh carefully the social and economic factors involved. There are obvious economic advantages in the outright purchase and complete ownership of land. Agricultural experiments and improved methods and the commercialisation of farming are easier where land is individually owned, and everywhere, in Europe in the past and in Africa in the present, the economic motive is a powerful force making for change. The social aspect of such change is apt only to be recognised later when the damage is done.

So far Nigeria has been fortunate in that its British rulers have prohibited the sale of land to non-natives. And the fact that native law and custom does not recognise sale is a great safeguard, Even now a fall in the price of palm oil is felt with great discontent by a bush village. Not only luxuries are curtailed but such things as school attendance become difficult. But at least people have the land with its means of subsistence. If this were to go a class of landless wage earners would grow up who would be dependent on the fluctuations of European trade and employment. Unemployment would become a practical issue. It is certainly a prospect to give pause to those who think in terms of social loss as well as in those of immediate economic gain.

v) This paper does not touch on the problems of land tenure in urban areas. In any case such problems have not yet arisen in Ibo country to anything like the degree in which they are present west of the Niger in such places as Lagos or Abeokuta.

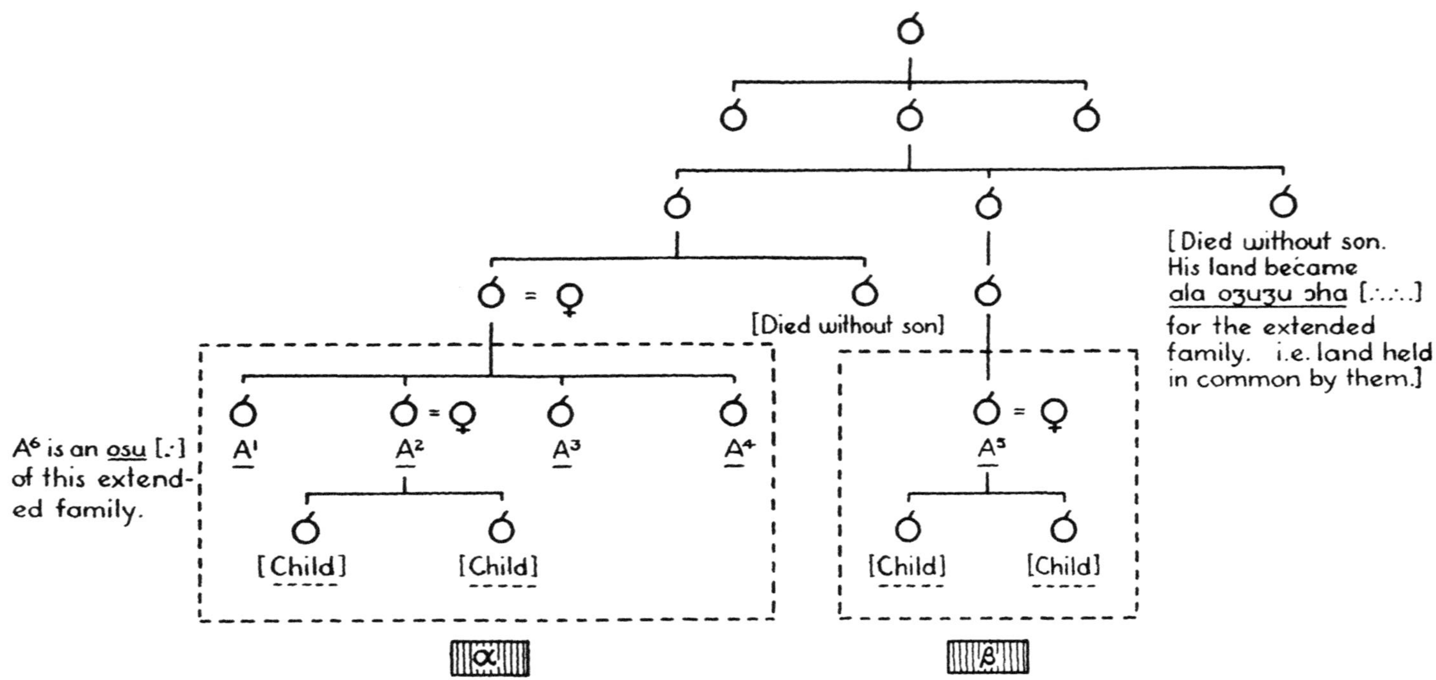

GENEALOGICAL TABLE OF MALES OF EXTENDED FAMILY A.

The dotted lines show the different land owning groups.

Below them is the hatching by which their land is shown in the large map of Umueke-ama division of Umueke village.

Living members of the land owning groups are underlined, children with dotted lines.

♂ denotes male. ♀ denotes female.

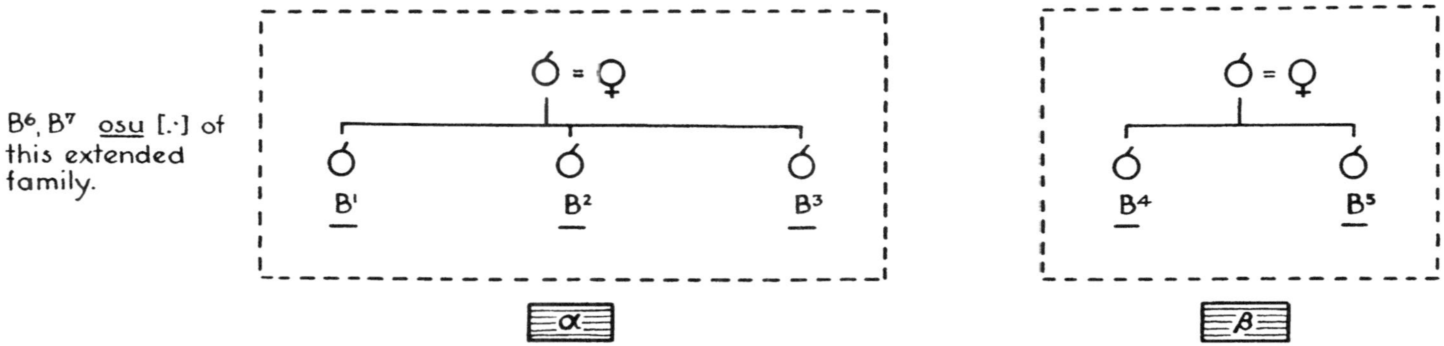

GENEALOGICAL TABLE OF MALES OF EXTENDED FAMILY B.

[Little information obtained. These are the only live land owning members.]

Key – as for extended family A. [See p. 38.]

Others Living with Extended Family C.

C8 – stranger who lived with this extended family.

c² – ♀ δ – widow of man who lived with this extended family and taken as one of them because his own relatives dead.

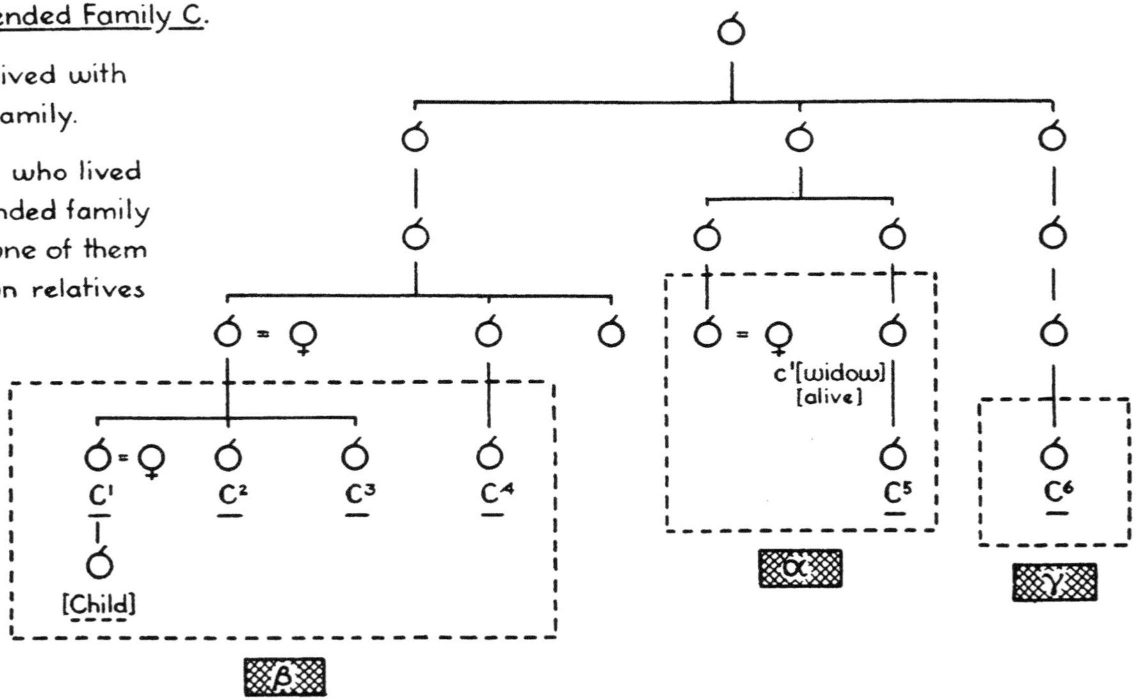

GENEALOGICAL TABLE OF MALES OF EXTENDED FAMILY C.

Key – as for extended family A. [See p. 38.]

♂ and large letter – C' – denotes male.

♀ and small letter – c' – denotes female.

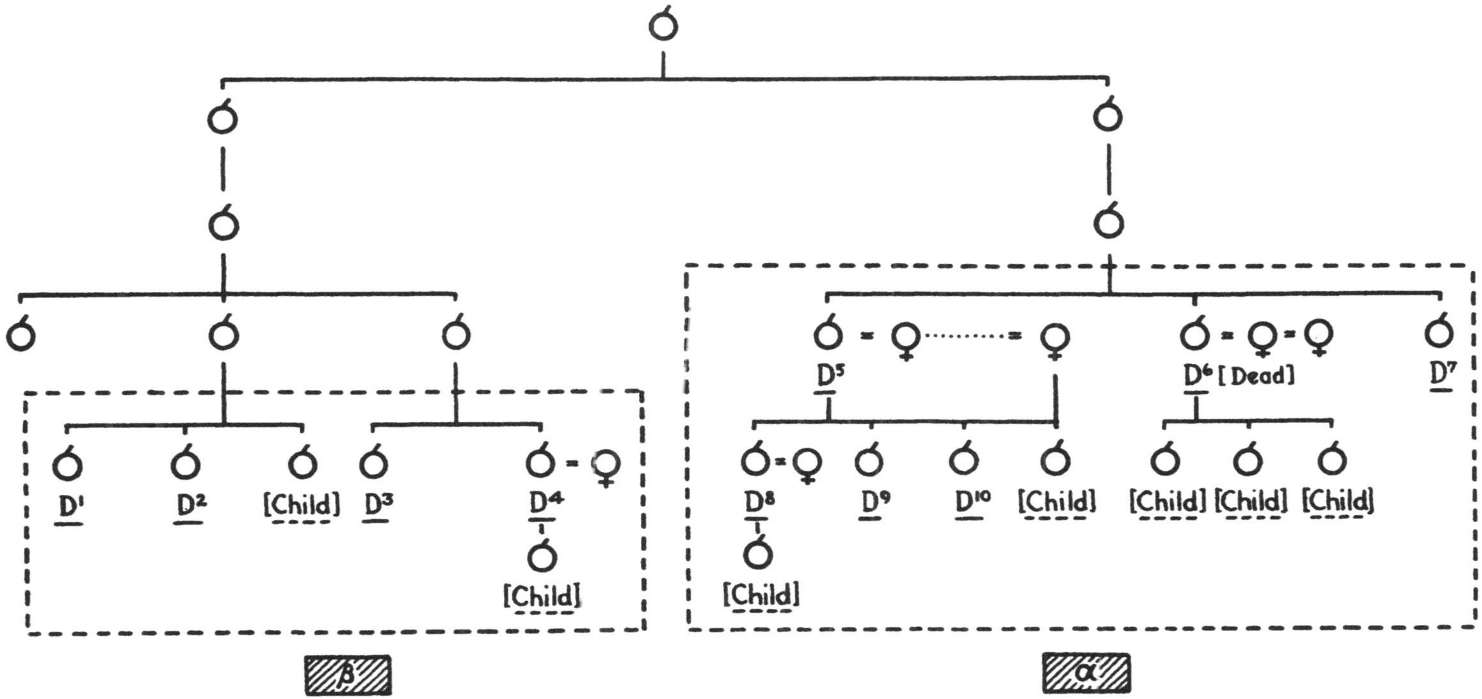

GENEALOGICAL TABLE OF MALES OF EXTENDED FAMILY D.

Key — as for extended family A. [See p. 38.]

ROUGH SKETCH MAP OF THE VILLAGE OF UMUEKE AGBAJA

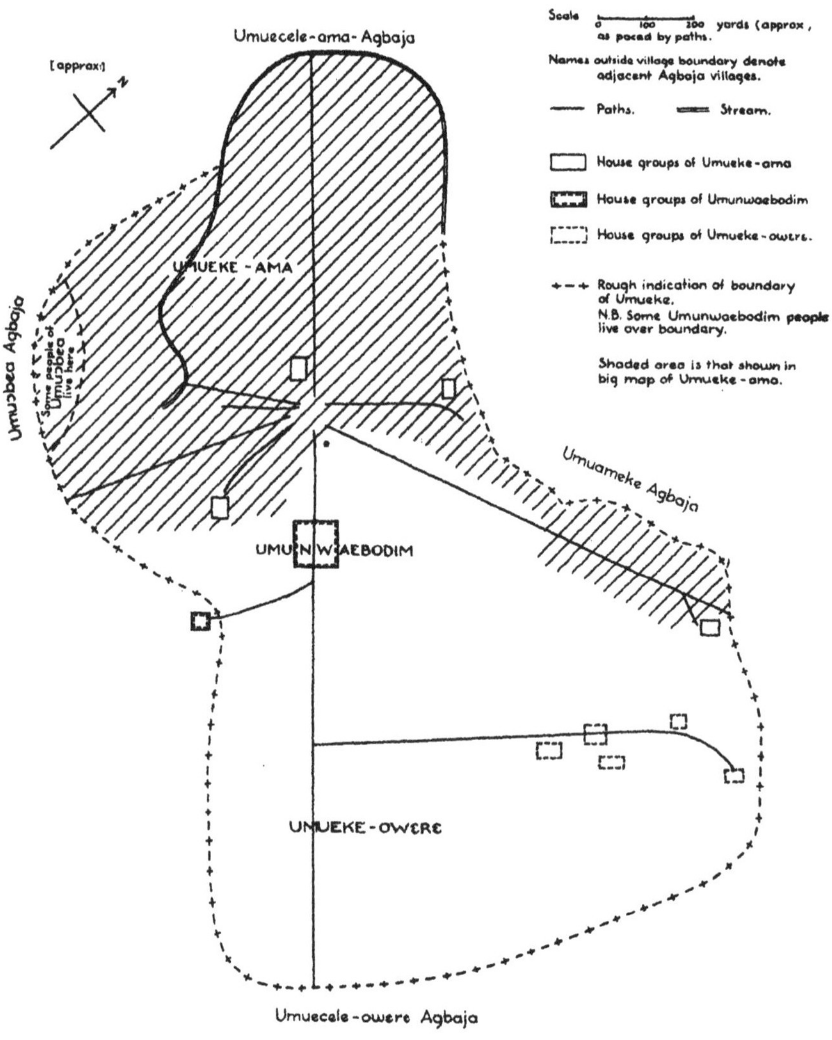

KEY TO NUMBERS IN LARGE MAP OF UMUEKE-AMA

1. 35 yards X 15 yards (approx:). Pledged by C^4 to a man of Umuobea village. An oilbean tree at one corner and an iroko at the other are boundary marks.

2. 62 yards X 20 yards (approx:). Divided for purposes of use between C^1 and C^4 though owned in common by their landowning group.

3. Shown for the farming season of 1937 to a widow of Umunwaebodim by extended family A. (I do not know which landowning group).

4. Pledged to C^8, the stranger living with extended family C, by the husband, now dead, of c^2.

5. 50 X 20 yards (approx:). (not quite rectilinear). Being farmed in 1937 by D^{10} who had been given yams by his father for the first time.

6. 50 X 20 yards (approx:). Being farmed in 1937 by D^8.

7. Pledged by father of C^1 to younger brother, same father, of father of A^3, who had inherited the rights over it since his father's brother died childless. A^3, in 1937, was farming the rectangle marked, which had been bush for about ten years. He had shown another piece of it to A^6, the OSU for farming for the season of 1937.

8. Pledged by one of the members of extended family C to a man of Umunwaebodim.

9. Pledged to D^5 by a member of extended family C.

10. A member of extended family C had 'shown' this land to a man of Umunwaebodim for farming for the season of 1937.

11. In hands of A^1 and ^{4} but whether inherited or got on pledge I do not know.

12. I was told a man of Umunwaebodim held this land but I do not know on what terms.

13. I saw a woman of Umunwaebodim farming here in 1935 but I do not know on what terms.

14. Shown by C^5 to A^4 for the farming season of 1937.

15. 33 x 43 yards. Land pledged by D^1 to an Umunwaebodim man in 1936 to raise money used in bribing the police. Being farmed in two plots by two kinsmen of Umunwaebodim in 1937.

16. 10 x 17 yards (approx:). Pledged as 15.

17. Being farmed in 1937 by a man of Umunwaebodim but I do not know on what terms.

18. Belongs to C^6, a young boy whose father was dead and who was the only surviving member of his landowning group. His mother had 'shown' this land to a man of Umunwaebodim for the farming season of 1937.

19. 40 x 50 yards(approx:). Shown by C^5 to a man of the neighbouring village group of Umunumu for the farming season of 1937.

20. Pledged by the father of C^6 to a man of Umunwaebodim who later paid more money for it in order to make it unlikely that the owner would redeem the land.

21. Pledged by extended family A (I do not know whether any special member) to D^6, now dead. On the land is the market shrine of the village deity. This would not be farmed over. Also it stands in the market clearing. I was told that ownership of land does not necessarily involve ownership of shrines on the land. They may have been put there by someone else.

22. Pledged by an elder 'brother', now dead, of D^5, to people of the next door village of Umuameke Agbaja.

23. Pledged by father, now dead, of D^5 to same people of Umuameke as in No.22.

24. Belonged to husband now dead of c^2. I was told, but did not confirm, that she had shown it for the farming season of 1937 to C^8, the stranger living with extended family C and that he, finding that yams grew well on it, had got it from her on pledge. (This point about widows without sons pledging or 'showing' their husband's land, needs following up. I have met it once or twice.)

25. Pledged by husband, now dead, of c^2, to people of the neighbouring village of Umuameke Agbaja. On it is the shrine of the female aspect of the village deity of Umueke. The women of Umueke perform annual rites here.

26. Pledged 'in old days' to people of Umuameke Agbaja, but I do not know by whom.

27. Land belonging to a man of Umueke-owɛrɛ. He 'showed' it to B^4 and B^5 for building their houses but himself farms on the land in front of the houses.

28. Pledged by father, now dead, of D^5, to same people as in No.22.

29. 104 X 22 yards.

30. 18 X 24 yards (approx:).

31. 68 X 25 yards (approx:).

32. Belongs to C^1's landowning group. Shown to an Umuɔbea man for season of 1935.

33. Writer's house.

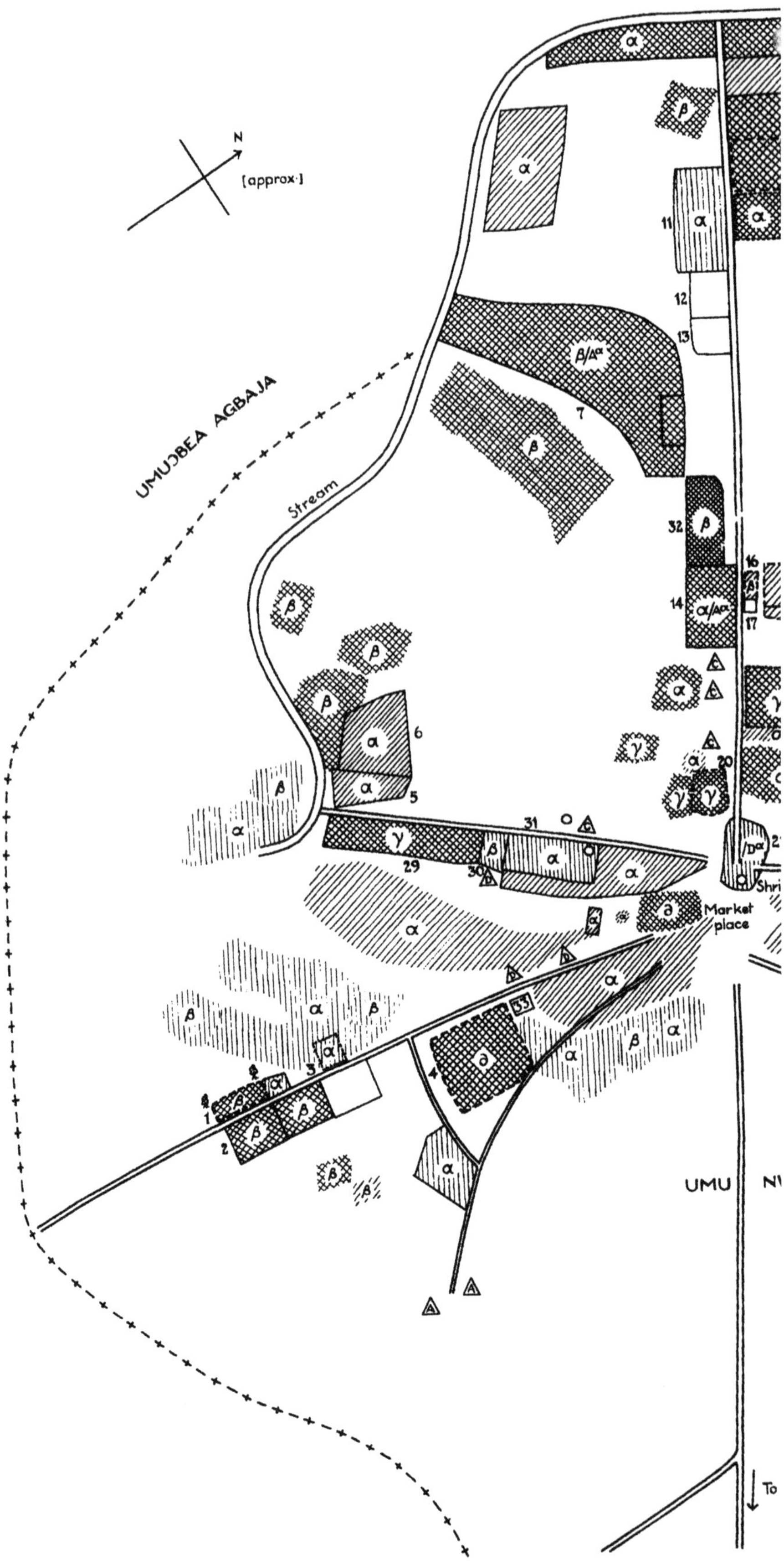
N
(approx.)
UMUDBEA AGBAJA
Stream
Market place
UMU
To

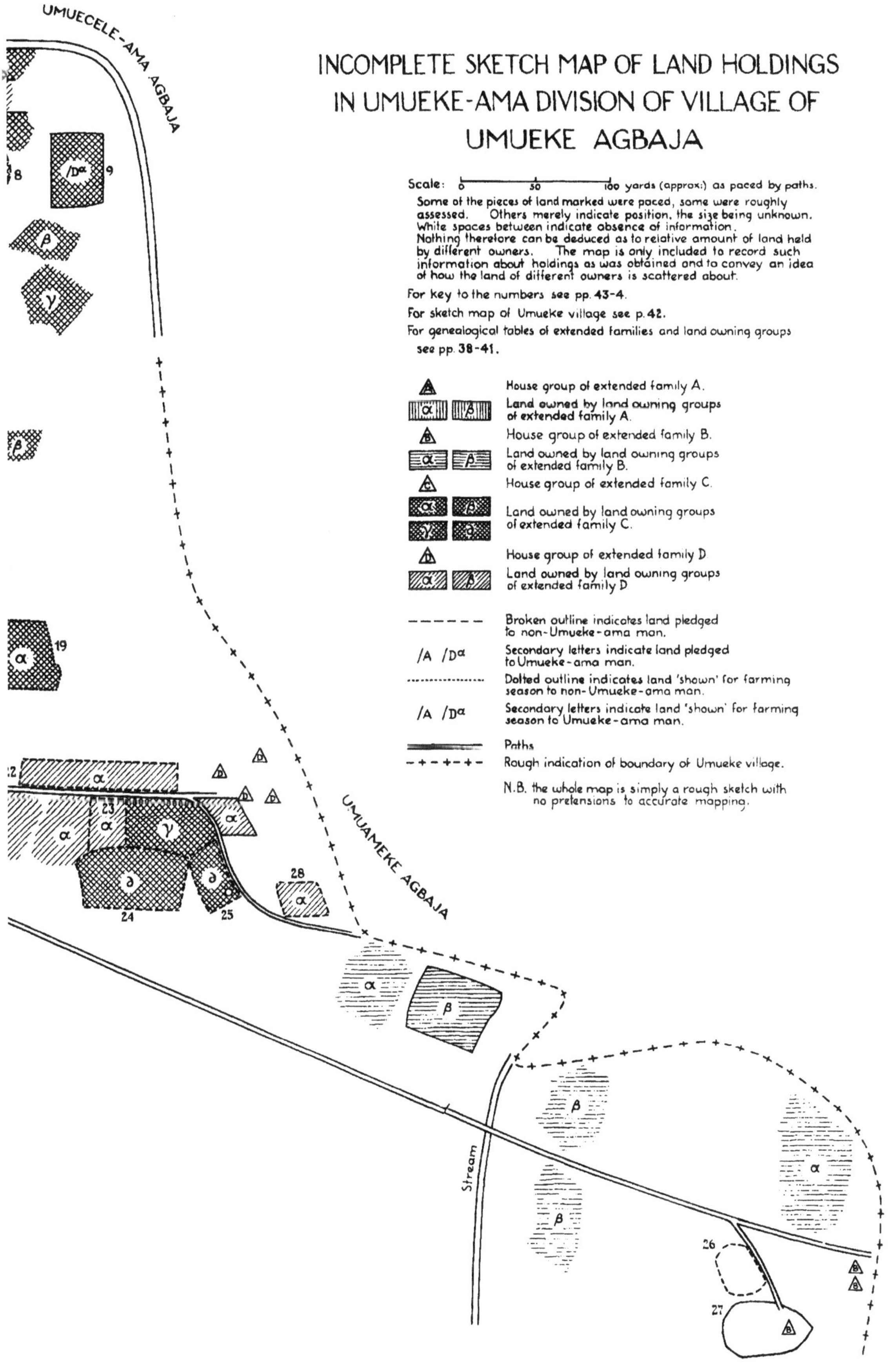
INCOMPLETE SKETCH MAP OF LAND HOLDINGS IN UMUEKE-AMA DIVISION OF VILLAGE OF UMUEKE AGBAJA
Scale: 0 50 100 yards (approx.) as paced by paths.
Some of the pieces of land marked were paced, some were roughly assessed. Others merely indicate position, the size being unknown. White spaces between indicate absence of information. Nothing therefore can be deduced as to relative amount of land held by different owners. The map is only included to record such information about holdings as was obtained and to convey an idea of how the land of different owners is scattered about.
For key to the numbers see pp. 43-4.
For sketch map of Umueke village see p. 42.
For genealogical tables of extended families and land owning groups see pp. 38-41.
House group of extended family A.
Land owned by land owning groups of extended family A.
House group of extended family B.
Land owned by land owning groups of extended family B.
House group of extended family C.
Land owned by land owning groups of extended family C.
House group of extended family D.
Land owned by land owning groups of extended family D
Broken outline indicates land pledged to non-Umueke-ama man.
/A /Dα Secondary letters indicate land pledged to Umueke-ama man.
Dotted outline indicates land 'shown' for farming season to non-Umueke-ama man.
/A /Dα Secondary letters indicate land 'shown' for farming season to Umueke-ama man.
Paths
Rough indication of boundary of Umueke village.
N.B. the whole map is simply a rough sketch with no pretensions to accurate mapping.
UMUECELE-AMA AGBAJA
UMUAMEKE AGBAJA
Stream
8
9
19
23
24
25
26
27
28

London School of Economics Monographs on Social Anthropology series
Series Editor: Charles Stafford

With over 70 volumes published since 1949, including classic work by Gell, Barth, Leach and Firth, the LSE Monographs now form one of the most prestigious series in the discipline of Anthropology. Presenting scholarly work from all branches of Social Anthropology the series continues to build on its history with both theoretical and ethnographic studies of the contemporary world.

74. Between China and Europe
Person, Culture and Emotion in Macao
Joao de Pina-Cabral

73. The Earth Shakers of Madagascar
An Anthropological Study of Authority, Fertility and Creation
Oliver Woolley

72. Chinese Sociologics
An Anthropological Account of Alienation and Social Reproduction
P. Steven Sangren

71. The Performance of Gender
An Anthropology of Everyday Life in a South Indian Fishing Village
Cecilia Busby

70. Arguments with Ethnography
Comparative Approaches to History, Politics and Religion
Ioan M. Lewis

69. Those Who Play with Fire
Gender, Fertility and Transformation in East and Southern Africa
Henrietta L. Moore, Todd Sanders and Bwire Kaare

68. Conceiving Persons
Ethnographies of Procreation, Fertility and Growth
Edited by Peter Z. Loizos and P. Heady

67. The Art of Anthropology
Essays and Diagrams
Alfred Gell (Edited by Eric Hirsch)

66. Leadership and Change in the Western Pacific
Edited by Richard Feinberg and Karen Ann Watson-Gegeo

65. Hierarchy and Egalitarianism
Castle, Class and Power in Sinhalese Peasant Society
Tamara Gunasekera

64. The Harambee Movement in Kenya
Self-help, Development and Education among the Kamba of Kitui District
Martin J. D. Hill

63. Society and Politics in India
Essays in a Comparative Perspective
Andre Beteille

62. The Power of Love
The Moral Use of Knowledge amongst the Amuesha of Central Peru
Fernando Santos-Granero

61. Making Sense of Hierarchy
Cognition as Social Process in Fiji
Christina Toren

60. The Social Practice of Symbolization
An Anthropological Analysis
Ivo Strecker

59. Gods on Earth
The Management of Religious Experience and Identity in a North Indian Pilgrimage Centre
Peter van der Veer

58. Ritual, History and Power
Selected Papers in Anthropology
Maurice Bloch

57. Sacrifice and Sharing in the Philippine Highlands
Religion and Society among the Buid of Mindoro
Thomas P. Gibson

56. Communication, Social Structure and Development in Rural Malaysia
A Study of Kampung Kuala Bera
William D. Wilder

55. Forest Traders
A Socio-Economic Study of the Hill Pandaram
Brian Morris

54. Ma' Betisék Concepts of Living Things
Wazir-Jahan Karim

53. White Nile Arabs
Political Leadership and Economic Change
Abbas Ahmed Mohamed

52. Knowledge of Illness in Sepik Society
A Study of the Gnau, New Guinea
Gilbert Lewis

51. Metamorphosis of the Cassowaries
Umeda Society, Language and Ritual
Alfred Gell

50. Choice and Change
Edited by John Davis

49. Beyond the Village
Local Politics in Madang, Papua New Guinea
Louise Morauta

48. Land and Family in Pisticci
J. Davis

47. West Indian Migration
The Montserrat Case
Stuart B. Philpott

46. Uncertainties in Peasant Farming
A Colombian Case
Sutti Ortiz

45. Pioneers in the Tropics
The Political Organization of Japanese in an Immigrant Community in Brazil
Philip Staniford

44. Political Systems of Highland Burma
A Study of Kachin Social Structure
E. R. Leach

43. Tribal Innovators
Tswana Chiefs and Social Change 1795–1940
Isaac Schapera

42. The Political Structure of the Chinese Community in Cambodia
W. E. Willmott

41. Report on the Iban
Derek Freeman

40. Time and Social Structure and Other Essays
Meyer Fortes

39. Take Out Hunger
Two Case Studies of Rural Development in Basutoland
Sandra Wallman

38. Anthropology and Social Change
Lucy Mair

37. Kinship and Marriage among the Anlo Ewe
G. K. Nukunya

36. Christianity and the Shona
Marshall Murphree

35. The Keresan Bridge
A Problem in Pueblo Ethnology
Robin Fox

34. Kinship and Social Organization
W. H. R. Rivers

33. Chinese Lineage and Society
Fukien and Kwantung
Maurice Freedman

32. Kinship and Economic Organization in Rural Japan
Chie Nakane

31. The Muslim Matrimonial Court in Singapore
Judith Djamour

30. Saints and Fireworks
Religion and Politics in Rural Malta
Jeremy Boissevain

29. Malay Peasant Society in Jelebu
M. G. Swift

28. Essays on Social Organization and Values
Raymond Firth

27. A New Maori Migration
Rural and Urban Relations in Northern New Zealand
Joan Metge

26. Kinship and Marriage in a New Guinea Village
H. Ian Hogbin

25. Conflict and Solidarity in a Guianese Plantation
Chandra Jayawardena

24. Legal Institutions in Manchu China
A Sociological Analysis
Sybille van der Sprenkel

23. Marsh Dwellers of the Euphrates Delta
S. M. Salim

22. Rethinking Anthropology
E. R. Leach

21. Malay Kinship and Marriage in Singapore
Judith Djamour

20. Social Status and Power in Java
L. H. Palmier

19. Political Leadership among Swat Pathans
Fredrik Barth

18. Lineage Organization in South-Eastern China
Maurice Freedman

17. Indigenous Political Systems of Western Malaya
J. M. Gullick

16. Studies in Applied Anthropology
Lucy Mair
Replaced by Volume No. 38

15. Two Studies of Kinship in London
Raymond Firth

14. Chinese Spirit-Medium Cults in Singapore
Alan J. A. Elliott

13. Changing Lapps
Gutorm Gjessing

12. The Chinese of Sarawak
A Study of Social Structure
Ju-K'ang Tien

11. The Ethnic Composition of Tswana Tribes
Isaac Schapera

10. Akokoaso
A Survey of a Gold Coast Village
W. H. Beckett

9. Tribal Legislation among the Tswana of the Bechuanaland Protectorate
Isaac Schapera
Replaced by Volume No.43

8. A Demographic Study of an Egyptian Province (Sharqiya)
A. M. Ammar

7. Housekeeping among Malay Peasants
Rosemary Firth

6. Land Tenure of an Ibo Village in South-Eastern Nigeria
M. M. Green

5. Marriage and the Family among the Yakö in South-Eastern Nigeria
Darryl Forde

4. The Political System of the Anuak of the Anglo-Egyptian Sudan
E. E. Evans-Pritchard

3. Social and Economic Organization of the Rowanduz Kurds
Edmund Leach

1 & 2. The Work of the Gods in Tikopia
Raymond Firth

For Product Safety Concerns and Information please contact our EU
representative GPSR@taylorandfrancis.com
Taylor & Francis Verlag GmbH, Kaufingerstraße 24, 80331 München, Germany

www.ingramcontent.com/pod-product-compliance
Ingram Content Group UK Ltd.
Pitfield, Milton Keynes, MK11 3LW, UK
UKHW050050200926
475702UK00019B/2761
* 9 7 8 0 3 6 7 7 1 6 9 6 7 *